PEANUT BUTTER
on my PILLOW

"Mother" and "Love"
differ only in name.
For miracles they work
are one and the same.
Happy Birthday, mom, Nov. 9, 1980
from Mary Ellen

PEANUT BUTTER
on my PILLOW
by
rita w. kramer

THOMAS NELSON PUBLISHERS
NASHVILLE

Library of Congress Cataloging in Publication Data

Kramer, Rita.
  Peanut butter on my pillow.

  1. Housewives—United States. 2. Mothers—
United States. I. Title.
HQ759.K7   306.8'7   80-12777
ISBN 0-8407-5724-7

To Gene, my partner and proofreader,
and to Kim, Maureen, Ross, Todd, Jon,
Jen, Josh, and Rory,
without whom there would have been
no peanut butter on my pillow

CONTENTS

ACKNOWLEDGMENTS

To the late Vienna Drake, former editorial assistant at *The Preston* (MN) *Republican,* and to Ron Wiltgen, former co-owner of that newspaper, who liked my early writing enough to publish it, thereby giving me the courage to attempt what has become *Peanut Butter on my Pillow*.

To Peter E. Gillquist for reading the first query letter I ever wrote.

To my Smith-Corona for its dependability through all my rewrites and erasures.

And most of all, to our dear Lord and Savior, who gave me the idea in the first place.

PEANUT BUTTER
on my PILLOW

chapter 1.

FROM HERE
TO INSANITY?

"Hey, Mom, Rory's playing in the toilet again!"

"Mom! Mom! Todd said if I don't find his fish hooks, he's going to dump water on my bed!"

"Mom, Josh is eating a big spoonful of something brown. It smells like peanut butter. He's sitting on your bed. He got some of it on your pillow, too, I think."

"Oh, by the way, Mom, Uncle Bob called while you were in town. He said they want to come down for the weekend. He said they were all packed up and would be coming as soon as they got all the kids stuffed into their station wagon."

It was ten o'clock on a Saturday morning.

"Oh, Lord," I asked, "is this the day I get to crawl

under the bed and have a nice, quiet nervous breakdown?"
"You know better than that," He shot back.
"Just checking," I said feebly.
No point in pursuing the subject. We both knew a cranial blowout wasn't on my list of options.

MISCELLANY OR MAYHEM?

In my forty-two years on this earth I've been through thick and thin; hell and high water; blood, sweat, and tears; and the agony and the ecstasy. (I've even tried to coin a fresh phrase). I've survived kindergarten potty lines, 4-H demonstrations, high school declamation contests, Inorganic Chemistry II, surgical waiting rooms, two solar eclipses, and a blind date. I've remained unruffled through a television debut (my own), eight no-turning-back trips through a labor-and-delivery suite, and scores of weekly newspaper deadlines.

In hair-tearing, how-did-I-get-myself-into-this potential, nothing has surpassed the daily routine of my primary occupation for the past xjlvpft-teen years as "technical supervisor" for my family's household. Call it domestic engineering, housewifery, homemaking, or voluntary imprisonment, if you wish. Newspaper columnist Peg Bracken wrapped it all up when she called it "the most miscellaneous of all miscellaneous businesses."

Keeping those miscellanies from turning to mayhem is the ultimate challenge of housewifery and motherhood. It's what this book is all about.

MARTHA, MY MENTOR

I was born nineteen centuries late. In the first century A.D. I could have had the mother of harried housewifery—Martha herself—as my mentor.

We might have had a back-fence chat about woman's work. I could have said one washday morning, "Martha, there's something I've been wondering about ever since I heard about the time Jesus scolded you for being a nervous Nellie. If Mary chose the only necessary thing, what are we supposed to do about the dishes? Who mops the bathroom when the toilet runs over? Who figures out how to get Magic Marker out of the drapes?"

But no Martha today. No mentor. I've turned repeatedly to Luke 10, verses 41, 42, to read: ". . . Martha, Martha, you are worried and troubled about many things. But one thing is needed, and Mary has chosen that good part, which will not be taken away from her."

Each time I've turned the page to find the rest of the story. Nothing. I've been forced to go straight to the top. I've learned to talk with the Lord Himself.

THEY DIDN'T TELL US EVERYTHING!

Back in my college home ec. years, each professor had her area of expertise. They never really explained how to get it all together.

There was the unclaimed jewel who taught Family Life, the size seven who tutored in pattern alterations, and the doctorate bachelor girl who had all the answers on household equipment. There was a folksy grand dame who led the way through floor plans and carpet samples, and a reasonably credible nutritionist who taught me more than I ever wanted to know about nutrition.

But at no time in my years of observation and ear-bending did one of them conjure up the courage to tell it like it *really* is, to explain what happens when you throw everything together in one house. My four-year curriculum came closest to authenticity with a lesson on childbirth in a home nursing class. In retrospect, I see the wry comparison: Were it not for the absence of a sanctified way out and/or a weak memory, would any woman present herself as a living sacrifice in an obstetrics ward? Likewise, would she take on housewifery?

Early in motherhood I decided to approach the problem of too much pressure and too little time with the "one day at a time" theory. I'd heard it mentioned in times of crisis, such as when the price of gasoline climbed above 27.9 cents per gallon, when frost touched Brazil's coffee crop, and when Grandma's house cat got diarrhea.

I saw no reason not to activate it against the harried (or is it "hurried"?) housewife syndrome, so one day I tried.

The next day I tried again. After two failures, I gave it another shot. Conclusion: "Not applicable."

Groceries are bought weekly, paychecks arrive monthly, gardens grow only in due season. I need to have more than twenty-four hours at a shot within control. A day at a time may work for bookkeepers, tailors, night nurses, Spanish monks, fighter pilots, and Sunday school teachers. It doesn't work for me. One can tread water only so long before being swallowed up by a tide that could have been anticipated.

TRY, TRY AGAIN

I adopted a new strategem, "a great morale booster," according to a magazine article. "Dress up for work," it said, going on to suggest spending the larger part of one's clothing budget on work clothes. Shower before starting the day, comb your hair and put on make-up, "even if it means getting up fifteen minutes earlier," counseled the article.

So I bought several pairs of smart denim jeans to replace the all-purpose residue of my premarital wardrobe, added an assortment of colorful tops equipped with handy pockets, and splurged on a half-dozen Maidenform marvels. New arch-support oxfords replaced my toeless tennies.

I meant business. I also had only $4.37 left in my annual clothing budget.

At five A.M. on Day One of my "Best Foot Forward" program, I woke to the gagging cries of a sick three-year-old. At six A.M., having cleaned up after the first crisis, I realized that an ice storm during the night had terminated our electrical power and our supply of hot water. "Cancel the shower," noted my cerebrum.

At 6:30, a sleepy-eyed two-year-old was discovered stuffing the last of the Charmin into the john. At seven the six-year-old announced, "I need some dry leaves for school today. We're gonna press 'em!"

Goodbye, Helena Rubenstein. I surrendered again.

SO MUCH FOR ORGANIZATION

Next, I contemplated the "worst first" idea. "Do your most distasteful chore first," the experts said. "Feel the triumph of a bad job done well—the rest will be easy," they taunted.

"Hogwash!" I thought each time it entered my mind. I could scarcely generate enough enthusiasm to open the refrigerator door, let alone clean the basement at the top of a morning.

Meanwhile, my ironing pile was threatening to avalanche. (This was two years B.P.P.—Before Permanent Press.)

Then I was struck by another old adage: "To fail to plan is to plan to fail."

"Of course it is," I thought. "How could I have forgotten? Aren't the management specialists always hammering at 'Plan the work, work the plan, plan the work, work the plan'?"

I made work lists. I organized them by the half-day, the whole-day, the week, the season. You name it, I had a plan for it. Was I organized!

Then, bingo! I was in the hospital, waiting for our four-year-old to come back from surgery. At home the beds were unmade, the garden peas were bulging in their pods, and a bamboozled babysitter was coping with three bewildered preschoolers.

"Lord, where have I gone wrong?" I asked in desperation. "I've learned all the rules. I'm healthy, I'm strong. I've got a dishwasher, automatic washer and dryer, a Posturepedic mattress, and a furnace that takes care of itself. Why am I such a good example of

18

'woman's work is never done'? What more do I need?"

"Try Me," He said.

"But I do. I *am,* right now."

"Sure you do—when you're in trouble! Why not *before* you start something? Come to Me first," He said gently.

"You mean like 'Seek first the kingdom of God. . . ?' "

" '. . . and His righteousness, and all these things will be added to you.' Exactly," He assured me.

"But," I protested, "I thought that meant if I go to church on Sunday I'll have the food, clothing, and other stuff I need for the rest of the week."

"That's part of it," He answered, "but 'all these things' also means things like peacefulness, efficiency, order, good judgment, wisdom. . . ."

"Then why am I still grasping and groping for those things? I go to church every Sunday," I pleaded.

"Because I put seven days into every week. You shouldn't expect one hour on Sunday morning to take care of the whole week. When I said, 'Seek ye first the Kingdom of God,' I meant *every* day. In fact, every *minute* of every day when you really get good at it."

"O.K., gotcha," I acknowledged, "but I'm a little dense. Just how do I go about it? Maybe you should spell it out for me."

"Will do," He said. (He seemed to be smiling.) "Number one, talk to Me first, before you do anything. Before you even start to plan. Get yourself up off that pillow at six o'clock. . . ."

"Six o'clock! Oh, Lord, no! At such an ungodly hour? If I get up that early, I'll never make it through the . . ."

"Don't interrupt. Do it the way I tell you, and I'll work out everything else. Remember: '. . . Do not be dismayed, for I am your God. I will strengthen you and help you . . .' (Isa. 41:10, NIV). After you've turned on a light and put on your spectacles, you can start reading my Word from one of your Bibles. Something from the Psalms is a good place to start the day. Then go to one of the Gospels. Add the day's selection from your devotional book if you want."

"But," I protested again, "I feel so yukky first thing in the morning. Morning mouth and all that, you know."

"Well, if it makes you feel better, go on down to the bathroom and freshen up first," He said. "While you're there, drink a glassful of cold water. Maybe a little fruit juice, too. It'll wake up your innards and give them something to do while they wait for breakfast. But don't take long. Ten minutes in the bathroom, fifteen in the Bible. That's your basic starter kit."

"Then what?" I asked.

"Then I'll make those other management theories start to work the way they're supposed to for you. Ask Me what to do with your day, and I'll help you make the plans. I'll make the work easier and more productive."

"Really?" I squealed.

"Hold it a minute! Don't get your expectations too high now. It won't happen overnight. You have to stay with it—you have to *grow*. A child doesn't become a grown-up in a day; a child of God matures by stages, too."

"But You *can* help me," I said expectantly.

"Yes, and I'll even throw in some joy and patience, and if you stick by Me, you'll get a good dose of cheerfulness, too," He promised.

"How can I lose? That sounds like a real bargain."

"I call it Love. See you in the morning."

I DIDN'T HAVE TIME TO PRAY

I got up early one morning
and rushed right into the day;
I had so much to accomplish
I didn't have time to pray.
Troubles just tumbled about me
and heavier came each task.
Why doesn't God help me, I wondered.
He answered, "You didn't ask."
I tried to come into God's presence,
I used all my keys at the lock.
God gently and lovingly chided,
"Why, child, you didn't knock."
I wanted to see joy and beauty,
But the day toiled on grey and bleak.
I wondered why God didn't show me.
He said, "You didn't seek."

I woke up early this morning
and paused before entering the day.
I had so much to accomplish
That I had to take time to pray.

—Author unknown

STEPPING INTO A BETTER DAY

- Rise thirty to sixty minutes before family. If necessary, apply Proverbs 6:9: "How long will you lie there, you sluggard? . . ."

- Brush or comb hair.

- Drink glassful of cold water and/or orange juice, preferably both.

- Brush teeth or use a mouth wash.

- "Wash up" or shower.

- Apply facial moisturizer and body lotion.

- Don a pretty robe or get dressed for the day.

- A dash of lipstick and light cologne won't hurt.

- Above all, spend fifteen to thirty minutes reading the Bible and praying about the day at hand, trusting Jesus to live in you and work through you. Read until you come to a personal message for you. Pray and listen until you have some work orders for the day.

- Say frequently: "Lord, help me to remember that nothing is going to happen to me today that You and I together can't handle."

chapter 2.

When "Clean" Is a Dirty Word!

Ever wonder what it would be like if Mr. Clean dropped in on you some day? I imagined that he paid me a visit once. Just once. He was uninvited, unexpected, and unwelcome.

"I noticed the fingerprints on your windows," he scolded as I answered his knock.

"Those are autographs of infancy," I countered.

"May I come in?" he asked, as he peered around me into the house.

"Enter at your own risk," I said.

"Yes, I see the toys on the floor."

"Tools of childhood," I explained.

His beady eyes scanned the living room.

"Now that I'm inside, I can see you've got a collection of cobwebs in that corner—and behind the drapes over there," he said accusingly.

"Spiders work nights," I said. "And it's honest work. How would you like to work all night and have somebody destroy it all with one swat in the morning?"

"And I suppose that closet there is a jungle of junk," he persisted.

"Could be. Never bothered old Fibber McGee," I shrugged.

He continued ruthlessly.

"You have all the symptoms of a person who probably has a mound of char in her oven, too. Right?"

"An honest by-product of the culinary arts," I said proudly.

"No doubt somewhere in your refrigerator there's a half-cupful of peas shriveling in an uncovered bowl," he nagged.

"Among others," I said evenly.

"Don't you care about ANYTHING?" he pleaded.

"I think I'm a reasonably caring person."

"Well, don't you know cleanliness is next to godliness?" he asked, struggling to hold back tears.

"Sir, I have no argument with godliness," I assured him, "but I don't get especially turned on by the cleanliness part, especially when there's a baby or two to rock and Little Golden Books to read. Tell me, why are *you* so hooked on it?"

"Because I believe in the Ten Commandments!" he said earnestly.

I dropped my Diaparene.

"Did I understand you correctly? Did you mean to

26

imply that 'Cleanliness is next to godliness' is one of the Ten Commandments?'' I asked.

"That's right."

"The Ten Commandments of the Bible? The Holy Bible?" I shrieked in disbelief.

"Well, isn't it?" he asked defensively.

"Nope," I said.

"It's *somewhere* in the Bible then" he said weakly.

"Not that I know of," I answered.

His eyes lit up. His enthusiasm returned.

"Shakespeare! Shakespeare said it! I always confuse the Bible with Shakespeare," he shouted, snapping his fingers in triumph.

"I doubt that, too. Guess again," I challenged.

A pause entered the conversation. I was tasting victory.

"How about the Lever Brothers?" he offered.

"Uh-uh."

"Procter and Gamble?"

"You poor antiseptic soul," I said softly. "Do you have a minute to spare before your next inspection? Let me tell you where that cleanliness-and-godliness thing really got started."

He nodded attentively.

"Well, it seems it goes way back to the Hebrew fathers. One Phinehas ben Yair apparently had been called upon to analyze religion. He came up with this summary—listen carefully now: 'The doctrines of religion are resolved into carefulness; carefulness into vigorousness; vigorousness into guiltlessness; guiltlessness into abstemiousness [that's a big word for sparing or abstaining], abstemiousness into cleanli-

ness; cleaniness into godliness.' Heavy stuff, huh? Are
you still with me?" I asked my guest.

"I think so."

I continued, "It was John Wesley who actually
spoke your treasured creed. In a sermon on dress, he
said, 'Cleanliness is indeed next to godliness.' He apparently got the idea from ben Yair. Francis Bacon had
been on the same track a couple of centuries earlier."

"Tell me more," he said dully.

"Bacon said, 'Cleanness of body was ever deemed
to proceed from a due reverence to God,' " I droned
onward.

"So then I'm right!" said my visitor.

"To a degree."

"To a degree? *To a degree?* But clean is clean.
Either you're clean or you're not!" He was beginning
to get testy again.

"But," I interrupted, "the question is: *How* clean
must clean be? And another thing—ben Yair, Wesley,
and Bacon were all talking about cleanness of the
body. I don't think they would have cried 'Heresy!' at
the sight of a dustball under the bed, do you?"

"You may have a point there," he conceded.

"Since you seem to respect the Bible, you might be
interested in a little gem that I delight in—you can find
it in Proverbs 14:4. *The Living Bible* says this one best,
I think."

"Out with it—the suspense is conquering my Right
Guard," he said impatiently.

"O.K., it goes like this: 'An empty stable stays
clean—but there is no income from an empty stable.' "

"So?"

"So that's why you can find fingerprints, cobwebs, last week's newspapers, and some dishes in the sink at my house when you drop in. Right now there's more 'income' from playing Candyland, kneading Playdoh, taking a romp out to look at the baby kittens, or discussing internal affairs with my husband than there is from chasing dust and stray Tinkertoys."

"B-but, but if the Lord thinks so much of goodness, truth, beauty, longsuffering, and diligence, it's hard to believe He doesn't care about cleanliness!" he pleaded again.

"He *does,* He *does,*" I reassured him. "But not so much about the kind of cleanliness that you've dedicated your life to."

"Prove it," he said, defiantly now.

"It's not for me to prove. Read His Word yourself. If He tells you a spotless house will get me into heaven, or that the lint behind my refrigerator will keep me out, just leave a Johnny mop and a bottle of Lysol on my back doorstep your next time around. I'll get the message."

I never heard from him again.

A MOTHER'S LAMENT

She stood apologizing at the door
before she let me in.
"There are babies' fingerprints
upon the pane," she said.
And as I stepped inside,
she lamented more:
"There are toys, I'm afraid,
all o'er the floor."
A pair of baby shoes
were in the hall.
She ran to pick them up,
lest I should fall.
I felt the tears stream down
my cheeks as I deplored,
"I have no baby toys on my floor."

—Coleen Nash*

*Used by permission

CLASSIFIED DIRT

According to students of housewifery, there are three kinds of dirt: (1) dusty dirt, (2) greasy dirt, and (3) clutter.

In my book, I divide it differently:

(1) Conquerable
(2) Bearable

Greasy invasions are conquerable. On the average day, dust is bearable. Clutter alternates between the two, depending on the circumstances.

Greasy dirt, under normal circumstances, rarely goes beyond the average kitchen. Two-legged peanut butter/jelly sandwiches caught slinking toward the living room TV can be drawn back with a few well-chosen words or, in the most resistant cases, a well-placed threat. Buttered toast, without exception, experiences a cold chill anywhere except at the breakfast table. Generally speaking, a squirt of Fabulous Four-in-One will put most misguided greasy invasions in their places.

On the other hand, dust is elusive. Just when you've coaxed it off a lampshade, you discover it gathered on the TV screen. Vacuum it from the drapes, and while your back is turned, your third-grader writes "Hi, there" in it on the top of the piano. In all-out warfare, it can be attacked with trusty Dust-No-More or a damp cloth, and you can feel like the honorable Harriet Homemaker—until the furnace sends out its next sooty snootful.

Chase dust from the East coast to the West. You won't catch it all. Save the effort!

With clutter, we get into some heavy decision-making. If magazines clutter the coffee table, that's a possible "bearable." If they're on my bed, that's different. If I pass an unmade bed on my way to close a four-year-old's sticky zipper, I can close that bedroom's door without suffering guilt pangs. But sneakers or bird eggs on a kitchen counter, or odiferous basketball socks on the dining room table, will be ushered to their assigned places without a second hearing.

PERFECTION ISN'T ALWAYS PRACTICAL

Planned neglect didn't come easily for me. (Oh, it happened regularly, but not because it was on my blueprints for happy housewifery.)

Through sixteen years of schooling, I dutifully dotted every "i," was always in my place with bright, shining face when the bells rang for class, and, as a class president in high school, was duly respected by forty-six assorted classmates. "Anything worth doing is worth doing well" was my byword.

Then came dishes and diapers. The babies dotted the walls with crayons. Their busy bottoms were congenitally resistant to toilet seats. Time control was of another world, and I was respected only by the local grocer. My previously valid creed was in for some mild-to-moderate adjustments.

LORD, SHOW ME THE SHORTCUTS

Being basically lazy, I gradually saw my new environment as a challenge to devise and develop a collection of shortcuts. This, together with building a supply of rationalized indifference, became an all-consuming goal.

The best ideas came when I expected them least. The bottom of the barrel tended to have the tastiest fare.

There was the washday morning when I complained, "Lord, there must be a way out of some of this. I've come to hate matching up socks so much that sometimes I just leave them jumbled in the clothes basket. Then the kids come barefooted looking for clean socks when the schoolbus is already barreling down the road. And I suspect that the washer is even swallowing some of them, because every week there are two or three that don't seem to have mates."

His answer was instantaneous.

"Clothespins!" He said. "Just clip each pair of socks together with a wooden, spring-type clothespin. The extra weight will keep the socks from floating out with the rinse water, and you won't have any matching to do. Better still, give the kids a supply of clothespins so they can clip their own dirty socks together when they take them off."

I tried it immediately. It works! It works! I praise the Lord for *that* big helper and for many more.

Sometime later, but not before I needed it, I found a postscript to that timesaver. When I began to have trouble distinguishing one boy's socks from another's,

I labeled the clothespins with permanent markers. It, too, *works*.

LET LOVE COME FIRST

On another day, the Lord tapped me on the shoulder and dropped another spark into my wilting brain.

"Who are you cleaning and polishing for, anyway?" I was saying to myself.

My self struggled to answer.

"Well, I know it's not for my neighbors. If it looks like I'm not such a hot-shot housekeeper, they can feel good because they're doing better. . . .

"And it's not for my friends. My real friends don't care—they like me anyway. . . .

"I doubt that I'm really doing it for my children. I probably work in *spite* of them, not *for* them. . . .

"My husband? Well, except for a few with "terraphobia," most husbands seem to be comfortable with the lived-in look. Mine seems normal in that respect. . . .

"I suppose I'd like to think I'm doing it for You, Lord."

"I knew it," He said softly. "But listen. My blood has cleansed your heart—that's the important thing. I loved you so much that I let my hands be nailed to a cross for you. Do you really think I would abandon you now just because you don't keep a showcase house at all times? There's a good reminder of how I'll stick with you in the ninth chapter of Nehemiah. Read it."

I promised to do that just as soon as I'd finished the dishes.

"I suppose I wasn't being completely truthful when I said I'm working for You," I confessed. "I'm doing it for myself, too, and sometimes I get *so mad* when I work so hard to clean the house and it's all messed up a little while later—or when nobody appreciates what I do."

"You remember that before I left the world to come home, I gave you one new commandment," He said.

"That we love each other as much as You love us, yes?" I said expectantly.

"Well, just *do* that," He said. "I put all of you together in that little cottage for a reason: First, to love each other unselfishly, then to help each other. Determine what makes your family happiest and do it. You may have to show the children how to love and how to appreciate what other people do, by your example. Sometimes husbands need the same example. If you get too much flack or if they take advantage of you, tell Me about it. I have ways of changing things."

"There's a catch in that," I said. *"How* can I tell what they want? Sometimes I think they don't even know themselves."

"This way: Make a list of the routine jobs you try to get done in a day. Describe each one a little. Then have your husband and older children rank them in importance. Rank them yourself, too. Then average your rankings and list them again, starting with the most important ones first. Just between you and Me, it might wake all of you to how much there is in running a home. And one thing more . . . try to remember *your house was made to serve you, not vice versa.*"

Housewifery was looking better.

"Lord Jesus," I prayed, "You're wonderful beyond words. I can't understand how You know me so well, or how You know so much about everything, or why You should even care about me and my bathtub ring. But I believe You, I trust You, I love You, and I need You. Help me keep first things first."

"Will do. Just knock when you need Me."

Cleaning and scrubbing
   can wait 'til tomorrow,
For babies grow up,
   we've learned to our sorrow.
So quiet down, cobwebs.
   Dust, go to sleep.
I'm rocking my baby,
   and babies don't keep!

—Author unknown

WHAT COMES FIRST?

Here's a goal-setting device I developed in my work as a home economist. Deciding what should come first in housewifery's daily chores is a family matter. Let each member of your family rank these nineteen items in order of importance to him/her: No. 1 for the most important, 2 for the next, etc. Then total and average across, and rerank to see what *your* family thinks should come first at *your* house.

	Rank in importance			Avg. Across	Our Ranking
	Mom	Dad	Children		
• Meals served at same time every day.					
• Homebaked cookies, cakes, or pies served regularly.					
• Table nicely set with good dinnerware and an attractive centerpiece.					
• Kitchen TIDY: Dishes done, floor swept or vacuumed, counters and appliances wiped.					
• Kitchen CLEAN: As above, but floor washed, appliances, cabinets, and windows gleaming.					
• Kitchen CLEAN BUT NOT TIDY: As immediately above, but dishes stacked in sink or dishwasher, a few items not in their places.					

PEANUT BUTTER ON MY PILLOW

	Rank in Importance				
	Mom	Dad	Children	Avg. Across	Our Ranking
• Living room TIDY: Newspapers,magazines, books, toys put in their proper places.					
• Living room CLEAN: As above, but furniture dusted (including up-holstery), wood furniture polished, floors cleaned, walls and drapery free of dust.					
• Living room CLEAN BUT NOT TIDY: As imme-diately above but may have some reading mate-rial, toys, or personal items lying about.					
• Bedroom TIDY: Bed made, pajamas put away, dresser tops orderly.					
• Bedroom CLEAN: as above, but floors cleaned and furniture dusted, mirrors and windows sparkling.					
• Bedroom CLEAN BUT NOT TIDY: As imme-diately above, but a few clothes, shoes, and per-sonal items not put away.					
• Bathroom TIDY: Towels hung, toothpaste and toiletries put away, no clothing present.					
• Bathroom CLEAN: As above, but fixtures and mirror gleaming, floor washed.					

WHEN "CLEAN" IS A DIRTY WORD!

	Rank in Importance			Avg. Across	Our Ranking
	Mom	Dad	Children		
• Bathroom CLEAN BUT NOT TIDY: As immediately above, but towels not hung neatly, some personal items in sight.					
• Homemaker well groomed: bathed, neat hairdo, fresh clothing, light makeup if desired.					
• Mom to drive family to school and community activities when needed.					
• Mom to spend as much time with family as possible, skipping any of the above in order to do so.					
• Mom to have some solitude each day: At least half an hour to use as she wishes—resting, reading, or pursuing a hobby or special interest.					

Rewrite the items here in the order your family ranked them:

1.

2.

3.

4.

5.

6.

7.

8.

9.

10.

11.

12.

13.

14.

15.

16.

17.

18.

19.

WHAT COMES FIRST IN OCCASIONAL JOBS?

	Mom	Dad	Children		Avg.	Our Ranking
● Mending and pressing done promptly.						
● Mom to do grocery shopping.						
● Sheets and towels ironed.						
● Closets and drawers orderly.						
● Gardening and weeding done by Mom.						
● Family's errands run by Mom.						
● School events participated in by Mom.						
● One or two community or church projects done by Mom.						
● Mom to have at least a few hours off each week to do as she pleases.						

41

Rewrite these nine occasional jobs here in the order your family ranked them.

1.

2.

3.

4.

5.

6.

7.

8.

9.

Here are some miscellaneous suggestions to save you time and effort:

• Appliance wax or surface renewers (available from kitchen appliance dealers) reduce time needed for cleaning appliances. Their long-lasting shine says, "I'm clean!"

• Buy the best, most powerful vacuum cleaner you can afford. A dual motor machine is a good investment—probably even a necessity for shag or plush carpeting.

- With weekly removal of leftovers and wiping of spills as they occur, most refrigerators will stay in bearable condition with a thorough cleaning done no more than once a month.

- In the difficult last weeks of pregnancy, barbecue tongs are a handy helper for pick-up chores.

- Put the toaster in a deep cupboard drawer and *use it there* to simplify after-breakfast cleanup. (Just be sure to keep the drawer open when you're making toast and unplug the appliance when done.)

- A breadbox or metal-lined drawer helps contain crumbs.

- Use terrycloth tablecloths. Buy them readymade or make your own from yardage. These are good spill-stoppers for young families.

- Grandma's aprons, made in today's fabrics, save on laundry and free the cook to be more creative because he/she need not be concerned about soiling clothing.

chapter 3.

ZPG,
GET OFF MY BACK!

"When they told me there was someone having her sixth up here, I expected to see an old lady," said the young, bearded hospital resident.

I'm climaxing a nine-month walk with Creation, and this fellow wants to discuss the science of aging, I thought.

"I'm nearly thirty-five. Is that old enough?" I mumbled from my end of the delivery table.

Unintelligible monosyllables filtered through his mask, and I sensed a generation gap spreading over that delivery room.

Is this one of those Zero Population Growth enthusiasts? I mused.

Meanwhile, the sleepy-eyed doctor detected a gap of another nature—a pause in my laboring.

"Come on, Mrs. Kramer, let's keep working. I'm getting uncomfortable sitting here on this stool."

"Want to trade places?" I offered with as much compassion as I could summon before calling for the gas mask.

The second hand on the Westclox on the wall floated around to 2:15 A.M., and a squalling, nine-pound baby girl was welcomed aboard. I had a new excuse for stocking Mennen Baby Magic, sweetest-smelling lotion this side of the diaper pail.

She was shuttled off to the nursery to complete her welcoming ceremony, the reluctant delivering officer scurried back to his night-duty cot, and I was bedded down under a heated blanket in a room where the very air I breathed seemed to be oozing satisfaction.

But should I have apologized to that young medic for exposing him to a deadly disease—multiple childbearing? Should I have slipped into my scuffies and tracked him down to offer first aid for shock?

No, 'twas better not to belabor the matter. He needed time to forget, time to sleep it off, to convince himself the experience had been but a nightmare.

THE LORD HOLDS VETO POWER

"Don't you know about birth control?"

It was our young former pastor speaking.

"I'd call it *conception influence,* but yes, of course, I know about it. In fact, I'm qualified to teach it in the right situation, if I wanted to," I replied with some puzzlement.

"But you don't believe in it."

"Oh, yes, I believe in it, but I think I see it differently than you do. I think our Creator is better qualified than I am to determine the size of my family. It's a long story, but He has told me quite plainly that, when "family planning" is practiced, He wants to be consulted regularly. I trust He'll tell us when we've reached our allotment."

"No, no," he shook his head in vigorous disagreement. "When God created the world, He gave us not only the power to reproduce, but to decide when and how much."

"I'm aware of that way of thinking and can understand the reasoning, but you can have the philosophy," I assured him. "God willing, I'll spoon the Gerber's."

"Why? When people all around you with greater fortunes are settling for one or two children, why are you going the opposite direction?" he quizzed me.

"I was propagandized by Ma and Pa Kettle and *Cheaper by the Dozen* at a very impressionable age," I teased.

"Is that a fact?" he said dryly.

"Perhaps. But seriously," I continued, "I know this may be hard to take, but early in my life, the Lord gave me the desire to have a large family and, later, a like-minded husband. As I see it, everything's working together for good."

"But what about this overpowering population explosion we're in? How can you justify it?"

47

"I'm told not to worry about such things—but I *pray* a lot. I figure if a sparrow doesn't fall to earth without God's knowledge, and if even the very hairs on our heads are all numbered, then surely He is controlling the population of this planet, too. He holds the future, and He holds me and my family. When it comes to controlling family size, I can scarcely presume to try, really."

He was not convinced. He was an immovable object—but so was I.

AN OPEN LETTER TO PLANNED PARENTHOOD:

Dear Planned Parenthood,

I wondered what you were up to. Now I think I know.

I didn't think anything of it when you drew little pictures of human reproductive systems and printed them in multiples for the world to study. I had already learned those things in biology class.

It didn't bother me when you developed basal body temperature charts. My doctor had the same tools in his office.

I wasn't alarmed when you printed illustrated booklets on contraceptive methods and passed them out at the county fair. This, too, was information readily available in doctors' offices and drugstores—and, somewhat disturbingly, at junior and senior high schools.

But I began to wake up when I learned that no one knows for sure how the IUD works, probably that it doesn't actually prevent the beginning of a new life but, rather, prevents the ovum from reaching a place to continue receiving nourishment—in other words, that it automatically induces abortion and is not a contraceptive. That's when I started to distrust you.

My skepticism grew when you declared that "the pill" is safer than pregnancy, while I personally knew women who had died of blood clots or who had developed life-threatening thrombophlebitis as a result of oral contraceptives.

Hostility began to swell in me when I had to fight a horrendous, lonely battle with low blood sugar after I briefly succumbed to the "virtually one hundred percent effective" cries of the pill pushers.

Even so, I did my best to ignore you when you began hammering on Zero Population Growth, filling loving parents with guilt.

And I didn't openly blame you, even when a doctor's first words after delivering one of my babies wasn't the customary "Congratulations!" but "Now what are we going to do about birth control?"

But when you opened abortion clinics to

make it easy for mothers to kill their babies, that's when I realized your whole philosophy *stinks.* You may not realize it, but it's the same mind-set that made the bed for Nazi Germany.

Planned Parenthood, take a leap!!

Whether you believe it or not, God is still the Creator! Who are *you* to try and tie His hands?

Sincerely,

Rita Kramer

DIARY OF AN UNBORN CHILD

March 19—My parents don't know it yet, but my life began today. I'm a boy, and my hair will be dark and curly just like my dad's. I'll enjoy football. Doesn't everybody?

April 5— I'm only 17 days old, but I've got my own blood cells now. My placenta is taking good care of me.

April 12— My heart is beating regularly now. It's so nice to know it will keep on beating all the rest of my earthly life.

May 1— Today my mom's doctor told her I am here. I can hardly wait to have her hold me in her arms.

May 7— Wow! This is really something. Electric waves are going through my brain and my fingers, toes, and ears are complete.

May 15— My mother decided she didn't want me. She killed me today.

HUGS AND PRICKLY HEAT

Motherhood isn't for quitters. The fainthearted ought not apply. Becoming—and remaining—a mother is a permanent event.

It means rinsing diapers when you could be hanging loose on Waikiki, settling into the La-Z-Boy at 3:00 A.M. to comfort a toddler with prickly heat when you're not so cool yourself, and watching Big Bird and Grover always but Barbara Walters hardly ever.

It's wishing there were another superhuman being in the house who answered to "Mom!" It's being paged in the ladies' room at the shopping mall because your three-year-old has slipped through two locked doors into the janitors' supply room.

It's standing helplessly as your sewing machine is engulfed by kneeless jeans and split-seam T-shirts, while your patterns for Designer Originals waste away in shopping bags from the Village Sew 'n Sew. It's eating off Melmac until you think bone china is something Oriental dogs use to clean their teeth.

It means chubby arms hugging your neck and sticky but trusting little fingers reaching for your help. It's the joy of seeing your heirs grow to adulthood without getting messed up on pot or booze.

It can be everything Helen Steiner Rice would say it is, and more.

MISSION: IMPROBABLE

Recently, after eighteen years of do-it-myself housewifery, I gained a part-time mother's helper.

In one interview a prospect said, "Now Mrs. Kramer, I'm not interested in a babysitting job. I want something with challenge. I want to be able to see that I've *done* something at the end of the day."

"Susan," I said, "I can't just promise you a challenge, I'll *guarantee* it. In fact, if you'll take the job, we—all ten of us—will work together to see that you face a distinct challenge each and every morning."

We did.

When she went on to other endeavors nine months later, Susan considered our vacuum cleaner among her best friends. She had learned to recognize twenty-three pairs of shoes and knew where to find each at the sound of a piercing "I can't find my shoes!" She spooned out drop cookies by the dozens, knowing full well that they would disappear before another dawn.

She patiently rearranged furniture after games of hide-and-seek and hoisted muddy toy trucks from the bathroom sink. She learned to look the other way in resisting the temptation to tackle a teenager's bedroom. She could ignore a two-year-old's temper tantrum with the perseverance of a seasoned grandmother.

She knew a disposable item from a tattered keepsake and learned how to stack the toybox so the high-demand Tootsietoy fourwheelers wouldn't always be on the bottom.

She had the grace to wait until she was in her car and

headed homeward before breathing a sigh of relief and whispering an ominous, "Oh, boy!"

She accepted challenge continually, but she could afford to. She was the only member of our household staff who got a paycheck every Friday.

A CHILD BY ANY OTHER NAME . . .

There ought to be a law. If a man doesn't completely agree with his wife's choice of names for their offspring, shouldn't he speak before the name is registered at the courthouse or forever hold his peace?

Early in my teen years, I decided on the name for my first daughter, should I have one. BeBe Shoppe, Minnesota's first Miss America, had been my idol since I was ten. I clipped every newspaper and magazine item I found about her and pasted them into a musty scrapbook with flour-and-water paste. When she married, my scissors were reactivated. When the first of her four daughters was born, I snipped again, but more than that: I latched onto the name she chose for her firstborn—Kimberly. A beautiful name for a beautiful daughter of a lovely Miss America. Someday I would use it, too, I decided.

Not too many years later, when our first child was announced to me with "It's a beautiful baby girl!" there was no question about her name—not in *my* mind, at least.

Today that infant is eighteen, has flowing brunette tresses, big brown eyes, and curly lashes. She is a creative seamstress, an efficient second cook, and an accomplished musician.

What does she answer to, thanks to her father's affectionate ingenuity? "James."

When Kimberly, alias James, was fourteen months, she became big sister to another little package of femininity. A postpartum discussion at my bedside produced an equally feminine name for the delicate dolly (based on the names of two favorite people in our lives)—Maureen Alice.

What do we hear today when her father addresses her? "Alvinus."

Another fourteen months passed, and the head of the household finally had someone on his team, our first son. A long search for a first name, plus an automatic choice of his father's name as his second, produced "Ross Eugene" on his birth certificate.

So handsome as a newborn that a friend was provoked to warn, "Cute in the cradle; homely at the table," this sixteen-year-old is still handsome, but a slender, studious, cautious youth.

His current nickname? "Big Al."

This boy had to have a partner, but eighteen months later, when another trip to the hospital was imminent, our name bank seemed to be dry. Not until he was about thirty-six hours of age was this Number Two Son finally tagged with Todd Emerson, causing his father to remark, "With a name like that, he'll have to amount to something."

He did—but what's the in-house monicker today for this student of the gridiron? "Lucille"—"Lu" or "Lucy" for short.

Four-plus years later, after time off for good behavior, I delivered a third son at the local birthing center. Christened Jonathan Wesley and obviously all boy since the day his Wee Walkers hit the linoleum, this young man goes to bed at night with "Eunice" ringing in his ears.

Another three years passed and there was a changing of the guard with the arrival of a pink-cheeked, brown-eyed sweetheart who took easily to ruffles and ribbons. The name Jennifer Rae was ready and waiting for her. Her label today? "Snoose."

A year later, another search for another name had begun. While ending a busy day by reading from the Book of Joshua, it came to me. Joshua! If it's good enough for a successor of Moses, it's certainly good enough for one of mine. A few weeks later, a husky little boy befitting the name joined our family.

When his father announced the event to a neighbor, she scolded, "Joshua! How could you do that to a little baby?" She needn't have let her blood pressure rise, for today, around home base, he's better known as "Cyrus."

Numero Ocho arrived at the end of the busy bicentennial year with no naming decisions made. "Rory" had surfaced as a good possibility for a first name, but what about the second? How about borrowing his grandfather's? Rory Lyle? . . . Rory Lyle . . . The rhythm isn't quite right . . . but a name book says Lyell (with emphasis on the second syllable) is an English variation of Lyle . . . Rory Lyell . . . O.K., sounds good.

Does this busy little hazel-eyed toddler respond to

the rhythm of Rory Lyell today? No, "Boots" gets better results.

If I live long enough, I may one day hear my mate call his children by names that don't ruffle my scalp.

On the other hand, my own epitaph will probably read: "Here lies . . . Maude? . . . Mabel? . . . Agnes? . . . What *was* her name anyway?"

MOTHERING A MULTITUDE

The mother of a multitude has some characteristics not always seen or experienced in small-to-medium families.

Multiple mothering requires that you stockpile hand-me-downs until you could open your own thrift shop. It's taking two carts and a husband to handle the overflow when you do your grocery shopping. It's never having a problem with leftovers because there aren't any.

It's wondering what happened to your tulip bed but knowing better than to ask. It's never being lonely, yet fighting for a moment of solitude. It's peeling potatoes until you rue the day Idaho joined the Union. It's wishing you could have just one roll of Scotch tape to call your own.

It's giving repeated thanks for the services of electricity, running water, Frigidaire, General Mills, an all-weather house, a healthy body, and the indefatigability of the Holy Spirit.

Mothering my multitude is the most demanding, yet when well done, the best-paying job I could ever hope to have.

56

THE MOST IMPORTANT PERSON . . .

on earth is a mother. She cannot claim
the honor of having built Notre Dame
Cathedral. She need not. She has built
something more magnificent than any
cathedral—a dwelling for an immortal soul,
the tiny perfection of her baby's body. . . .
The angels have not been blessed with such
a grace. They cannot share in God's
creative miracle to bring new saints to
Heaven. Only a human mother can. Mothers
are closer to God the Creator than any
other creature. God joins forces with
mothers in performing this act of creation. . . .
What on God's good earth is more
glorious than this? to be a mother?

—Joseph Cardinal Mindszenty

PSALM 127

Unless the Lord builds the house,
    its builders labor in vain.
Unless the Lord watches over the city,
    the watchmen stand guard in vain.
In vain you rise early
    and stay up late,
Toiling for food to eat—
    for He grants sleep to those He
        loves.
Sons are a heritage from the Lord,
    Children a reward from Him.
Like arrows in the hands of a warrior
    are sons born in one's youth.
Blessed is the man
    whose quiver is full of them
They will not be put to shame
    when they contend with their
        enemies in the gate.

chapter 4.

THE HURRIER
I GO . . .

I never met the man, but I recommend G. K. Chesterton for a posthumous honorary membership in Housewifery, Unlimited.

This turn-of-the-century sage wrote, "One of the great disadvantages of hurry is that it takes such a long time," proving beyond doubt that he was one of us. He obviously prophesied how it would be when you're already ten minutes late for your dental appointment and you notice your fuel gauge stuck on the backside of empty. He could have imagined the feeling in your bones when it's six-thirty, the guests are due for dinner at seven, and you've just spotted the baking potatoes in the sink where you dumped them just before the phone rang an hour ago.

He foresaw the internal upheaval when you've overslept, but your schoolbus driver hasn't. He predicted what it would be like when you've delayed your trip to the hospital because you thought it was just another false alarm.

Mr. Chesterton may never have cleaned an entire house in fifteen minutes after his mother-in-law phoned in a "Surprise!" from the bus station. But he certainly would have understood the trauma of those who have.

GETTING UP IS UNDERWHELMING!

"Morning! It starts every day too early, not always brightly, and too often with scurrying designed to seed hypertension in even the most placid body. *Those* are the times that try mothers' souls." I was philosophizing again.

As always, the Lord was eavesdropping.

"That's one reason I told you to start your days by getting up early and coming to Me first," He volunteered.

"And that's why I'm working at it," I answered, "but it's not easy."

"No, it isn't, but do you remember your college home management house?"

"Could I forget it? I lived there for five weeks, supposedly to learn how to manage a home. And I do have fond memories of that place. But life was simpler then. Oh, to have an upstairs maid, a laundress, and a budget manager today."

"You realize it wasn't an ideal teaching situation for

real family living," He said, "but it had a few good things going for it. Remember how you'd go out on a date and then set the table for breakfast when you came in, just so you could sleep a little longer in the morning? You can still do that."

"My husband would be a bit upset," I warned. "He tends to get a little jealous about things like that."

"You know what I mean!" He countered abruptly.

"Sure—just kidding. You meant I could set the breakfast table before I go to bed—but my brain goes off duty before the supper dishes are done," I whined. "Any thought waves left in my skull after that are concentrated on getting my bones between the bed-sheets."

"I understand," He said sympathetically, "but setting a table doesn't take much brainpower, and you'll enjoy it more in the evening than if you have to do it under pressure in the morning. In a few more seconds, you could check that you've some butter or margarine out to soften for the toast—and see if you need to take another can of juice from the freezer. Even setting a pan on the stove for the scrambled eggs can help. Then morning won't come with such a jolt."

"But wouldn't it be a lot easier just to skip. . . ."

"And by the way," He went on, "all of you should have a high-protein breakfast, but don't think you have to stand over hot coils every morning. That oatmeal and eggs and bacon stuff is nice, but a breakfast of orange juice, peanut butter on toast, and a glass of milk has something from each of the basic four foods. It'll do the job. Think about it—don't forget to ask Me to help—and I know you can come up with some quick and easy complete breakfasts, things the kids can even put together themselves if you make the food available and lend a hand. Good experience for when they'll be on their own, working, or going to school. They'll be less likely to skip breakfast if they have a memory of Mom's morning mini-miracles to go on."

"Mr. Kellogg says a good day starts with breakfast, but I gather you're saying it can start the night before," I concluded.

"Just trying to help," He said. "Sleep in peace."

RECIPES FOR THE DAY'S MOST IMPORTANT MEAL

Here are some ideas for quick and easy breakfasts—admittedly odd but nonetheless edible. Add other foods from the Basic Four as needed.

Baked custard (made day before)
Grilled peanut butter or cheese sandwich
Denver (fried egg) sandwich
Pizza
Soft custard (made day before) over fruit (berries, peaches, etc.)
Rice pudding
Cottage cheese with fruit
Nut bread, plain or toasted
Cheese and crackers
Toast with peanut butter or cinnamon and sugar.

Try this meal-in-a-glass on those mornings when

time is short or when a toddler (or teen) refuses his scrambled egg.

BANANA BREAKFAST SODA

1 egg
1 cup orange juice
1 small ripe banana, sliced
1 Tbsp. honey
1 scoop ice cream

Spin in blender for about
fifteen seconds. Enjoy!

MOVING INTO PRIME TIME

It seems to be common knowledge that everyone has a high-energy "prime times" and low-energy "tired times." Wise managers use their prime times for their most demanding jobs.

My tired times used to be obvious, numerous, and sometimes virtually uninterrupted. But a *prime* time? I never found one. Well, maybe once or twice a month I'd get revved up about something, but I always had the impression it was something that's supposed to happen at least once a day.

Then came the winter afternoon when I found myself a stranded stranger in a snowbound city. I browsed through a book display in one of those soup-to-Santa Claus "drug" stores. Paperback westerns, mysteries, and romances were in abundance. *The Tryst on the Back Forty, Aunt Agatha's Affliction, The Year of the Dogwood,* and so on they went, pulp after pulp.

A hardcover number caught my eye: *Diet Away Your Stress, Tension and Anxiety: The Fructose Diet Book,* by Dr. J. Daniel Palm.

"Oh, come on, Doubleday," I thought, "how melodramatic can you get? Anything to sell a book!"

I bought the book. It has proven to be one of my best literary investments, one of my greatest godsends ever. One of the several hazards of housewifery is the "tired housewife syndrome." As in all people, no matter what their occupation is, this tiredness can be caused by spiritual starvation, self-centeredness, resentment, covetousness, or unresolved guilt, and those things must be dealt with in the realm of the spirit. We've a whole Book to help us. But too often fatigue is caused by an undiagnosed physical condition, low blood sugar, a biochemical upset that, in my own experience, was apparently triggered by my use of an oral contraceptive. Here's what I learned through Dr. Palm's work:

• Stress is all around us. Weather changes, telephones, bacterial and viral infections, frustrations, deadlines, noise, the nightly news, ornery neighbors, offensive traffic—all put stress on the human body.

• All varieties of stress cause an automatic and immediate stress response in the body, a biochemically-controlled set of physiological changes within the body's various systems.

• "Most people . . . are continuously responding to

stresses of one variety or another, but they do not recognize the signals.'' (See p. 49 in Palm's book.)

● Stress is additive; the body doesn't discriminate between the various causes, but more or less piles one on top of another.

● One's ability to withstand stress is hereditary but can be altered.

● *Hypoglycemia* (low blood sugar) *is a stress* caused by the body's response to glucose, sucrose, and other refined carbohydrates. It is perhaps the most prevalent and unnecessary stress of all in many persons.

● Hypoglycemia is one of the most frequent causes of not only fatigue, but irritability, tension, depression, insomnia, inability to concentrate, circulatory disorders, and internal agitation. It can result in alcoholism, obesity, hyperkinetic behavior in children, and suicidal tendencies, and is a common cause of migraine headaches, low sex drive, premenstrual tension, and craving for sweets.

● The body's use of fructose (fruit sugar) is such that, when fruit sugar is substituted for sucrose, glucose, and other sugars—and for refined carbohydrates such as white bread—it can virtually wipe out the above disorders. (Dr. Palm says overseers of the Olympics have supplied fructose for energy to contestants in the past few games.)

● "The public seems to be ahead of the medical profession in understanding not only the incidence, but the importance and manifestations of this widespread and frequently undiagnosed condition. There is even *opposition* to the concept by certain academic segments of the medical profession. This opposition seems to stem primarily from a lack of clinical experience because it can be easily demonstrated that a sizable percentage of patients responds dramatically to elimination of ordinary sugar from their diets. Similarly, many normal people experience considerable benefit from such a diet change and report that they experience *less fatigue, irritability, sleeplessness* and *variation in their daily energy level.*" (Italics mine. See p. ix in Palm's book.)

My own blood-sugar-battle story is long and complicated, but that last paragraph of Dr. Palm's pretty well sums up my own experience.

I searched out a supply of fructose, and within less than twenty-four hours after beginning to substitute it for other sweets in my diet, I felt like dancing and singing and telling the world about my discovery.

So I am!

SOLVING THE ENERGY CRISIS

I've been forced to learn a few things about energy and blood sugar control in the past ten years. In accordance with current knowledge on the subject, this is what I do to keep my blood sugar at optimum working level, fueling my body and brain with relaxed vigor.

I avoid: all candy (unless it's loaded with nuts)
        jams
        jellies

syrups
pie
cake
cookies
pastries
soft drinks
macaroni
noodles
spaghetti
potatoes (except in small amounts)
rice (except in small amounts)
alcohol
caffeine
aspirin
tranquilizers.

On the positive side, upon rising each morning I take two, two-gram fructose tablets and drink a small glass of unsweetened orange juice (fructose crystals or syrup stirred into the juice could substitute for the tablets, but I prefer my orange juice "natural"). I take one to three fructose tablets every two or three hours during the day and limit snacks to unsweetened fruit juice, fresh fruit, and cheese. For a super good night's sleep, I have a bedtime snack of orange juice and one or two fructose tablets or an equivalent amount of crystals or syrup. Fructose is available in tablet, crystalline, and syrup forms in most health food stores and at some drugstores.

THE DEVIL DELIGHTS IN DOMESTIC MAYHEM

If the road to hell were paved with good intentions,

there'd be a four-lane freeway through my living room.

"Lord, you know I'm trying to do the best job I know how here," I fumed, "but the interruptions, the distractions, the children, the phone, the daydreams, the hole in my vacuum bag, the birdbath salesman. . . ."

"Dear one, God did not give you a spirit of timidity, but a spirit of power, of love, and of self-discipline. Some of those 'interruptions,' especially those concerning your children, are just part of your calling. Beyond that, let me remind you that your adversary, the devil, is always stalking about, seeking to devour you," the Lord told me.

"Yes, but does he hide my broom and spill salt into the cookie dough?"

"You'd better believe it!" He assured me. "Not only would he like to see you throw in the towel on Me, but he works like you-know-who to get you discouraged, irritable, and busy-busy-busy with petty concerns, just to draw your eyes off Me."

"Uh-hum . . . I get the picture," I murmured.

"And anyone *in* that picture is a poor witness for Me—or a hypocritical one at best. The more inefficient, short-tempered, flippant, or sarcastic he can make you, the less likely that you'll lead anyone to Me. If your children can't see love and patience in you, they'll have a hard time seeing Me, too. Make no mistake, poor old misguided Satan dances because of domestic mayhem."

"I didn't know he was that diversified," I admitted. "I always thought he was a rather lazy chap."

"How'd you figure that?"

"Well, You know how we say, 'Idleness is the devil's workshop. . . .' "

"Ah, that it is, but busyness is no better. He'll use idleness to get you into trouble, but he uses busyness to pull you off target, too. When you can't go to a prayer meeting or rock the baby or read a good book or take a moment alone just to listen to the still, soft voice of your Lord because you have to polish the silver and sweep the basement and weed the garden and polish the doorknobs and run to another meeting, Satan's in his glory."

"He's *that* diligent," I said in dismay.

"What's more, he's against everything worthwhile. He's antifamily, antichildren, antimarriage, antichurch—against everything where real love can grow and where God's true Word can be taught."

"So what's there to do about it?" I asked.

"I've defeated him, and I've given you the authority to do the same thing. Just say, 'Satan, in the name of Jesus Christ, I command you to get away from me.' He'll run for the showers."

"O.K., so I get rid of that negative influence. Isn't there something more positive I can work with?"

"There's a solution as old as time," He said. "Just believe Me when I tell you that you can do everything I would want you to do through My power that is in you. Ask for a fresh touch of the Holy Spirit when your self-discipline is fading."

"Anything else?"

"Only one for now: Don't quit when you're down.

Just leave your hand in Mine, hang in there, and when the clouds are gone, you'll realize a blazing Son was working to clear them away."

THE PAUSES THAT REFRESH

I married a master of the postprandial nap. In fact, he's not so bad at the preprandial nap, nor even the intraprandial siesta when lunch is "bologna sandwiches again."

Although wifely devotion has sometimes persuaded me to prepare myself to discuss the internal affairs of Indochina or to reflect intelligently on the Taylor-Burton remarriage, lunchtime is usually not a mind-expanding event at our home. After some years of one-sided noontime verbiage, when my spouse's nodding had converted to fullblown snoring, I decided to enter the can't-beat-'em?-join-'em society. I claimed a spot on the couch and hoped for a fifteen-minute interlude uninterrupted by kith or kin.

Ah, the pause that refreshes, I learned. No wonder Sir Winston Churchill and John F. Kennedy and others survived the pressure cooker. They, too, knew the secrets of the mini-nap:

1. Choose a practical time.
2. Decide how much time you can afford to spend napping.
3. Set a timer.
4. When your time's up, *get* up!

If rest is important to being relaxed, so is exercise.

70

Housewives move around a lot, but we don't necessarily get enough exercise. A brisk walk or other regular activity in fresh air prepares the body, and very importantly, the brain, to work more efficiently.

A FRIEND IN TIME

"Next to Me, time is the most dependable resource you have."

"I don't think I heard you right," I said. "Say that again, Lord."

"Next to Me, time is your most dependable friend," He paraphrased.

"That's what I thought you said. But time a resource? Dependable? A friend?"

Time grays your hair, rounds your shoulders, blackens your picture tube. It wears out your carpets, crumples your mattress, and takes away your parents and children. He was telling me time is my friend?

"Well, imagine your predicament," He explained, "if there were no time at all—there'd be no life either, of course. Or suppose time actually passed faster some days than others."

"I see . . . yes, I suppose a cake would bake in seconds when clocks were creeping, but could be in the oven half a day when the hands were flying."

"So if you feel harried and helpless now, imagine the chaos you'd have if time weren't so dependable."

"But still, You'll have to admit it can get away from a person," I persisted.

"Not so easily if you make your wristwatch part of your work wardrobe. Strap it on when you dress in the morning, and don't take it off until you go to bed at night."

"But isn't clockwatching a no-no?" I asked, remembering a job orientation class back in high school.

"Not when you're working for Me. I give you a new supply of time every morning, and I like to see you use it well, getting a good balance of your top-priority items accomplished. You can help Me help you by keeping your eye on the clock."

Naturally, He was right again. His time was my time; but when I let my time become His time, He gives me better mileage. Hallelujah!

PLANNING PRIORITIES

Planning how and when to do jobs usually saves time, energy, and aggravation on the job. With the Lord as a planning partner, the benefits are multiplied manifold.

By far the best weekly and daily planning guide I've seen is Linda Dillow's *Priority Planner,* published by Thomas Nelson. It's superior because it's based on spiritual priorities.

The book consists of blank pages (you fill them in by the week) with those God-given priorities—the Lord, husband, children, home, yourself, and "outside the home"—each listed with an appropriate verse of Scripture as reminders to keep the priorities visible. It includes space for each week's menus and even tear-off shopping lists!

A MOTHER'S PRAYER

Oh give me patience when tiny hands
Tug at me with their small demands.
And give me gentle and smiling eyes;
Keep my lips from sharp replies.

And let not fatigue, confusion or noise
Obscure my vision of life's fleeting joys.
So when, years later, my house is still
No bitter memories its rooms may fill.

—Author unknown

I WILL NOT HURRY

I will not hurry through this day!
Lord, I will listen by the way,
To humming bees and singing birds,
To murmuring trees and friendly words;
And for the moments in between
Seek glimpses of Thy great Unseen.

I will not hurry through this day,
I will take time to think and pray!
I will look up into the sky,
Where fleecy clouds and swallows fly;
And somewhere in the day, maybe
I will catch whispers, Lord, from Thee!

—Ralph Spaulding Cushman*

*From *I Have a Stewardship* by Ralph Spalding Cushman. Copyright renewal © 1967 by Maud E. Cushman. Used by the permission of Abingdon Press.

chapter 5.

A PLACE FOR EVERYTHING?

Someone had named it Honeymoon House. Little did he or she know.

When we moved into this house twenty years ago with our Swedish glassware and matching sheets and pillow cases, like most of its more recent residents we were newlyweds. But we were different. We came to stay.

Today we're a five-bedroom family in a four-bedroom house. We think we've proven—to ourselves, at least—that it's possible for an "oversized" family to remain civil and reasonably presentable with but one small bathroom, plus a basement shower spigot at our disposal.

It isn't that the old Honeymoon House has stood

still while we stuffed it to capacity. It has submitted to major and minor surgery just to make way for the Kramers. Thanks to a landlord able and willing to wield hammer and saw or to call in the carpenter, Honeymoon House has had a facelift. We promised we wouldn't tell, but when our country's revivified former First Lady told of *her* face-lift, I decided Honeymoon House could bare her past, too.

The first operation began a half-dozen years after our arrival, when we numbered but six. A large upstairs bedroom accepted built-in wardrobes, a dresser, and study area—with no signs of postoperative rejection—and double windows replaced a single porthole. Wooden wall paneling completed the treatment.

Unalterable external construction of the room required that a fourteen feet by two feet space be left behind the wardrobe/dresser, a delight to this writer, the tenuring housewife. This accidental storage area now unobtrusively houses a collection of seasonal supplies and unforgettables.

Two years later, internal pressure was increasing again. Our "what-would-we-do-without-it? catchall, The Attic, was forced to become a living, breathing part of the house—our fourth bedroom. Located on the second floor and adjacent to two other bedrooms, it was more than a means of support for pigeon droppings. It had become The Attic because of its unfinished condition and the array of matter that found its way through the door—the magazines that "we might read some day," the high school letter sweaters, the gift boxes with assorted shreddings, the "courtship correspondence," and a proliferation of "junque."

A bale of plasterboard and a week of carpenters plodding through the house with T-squares and moldings turned it into what split-levelists would instinctively recognize as The Master Bedroom. With twin closets, cozy burnt-orange drapery, and a locking door latch, it's the best room in the house.

The year following the tenth anniversary of our invasion, Honeymoon House's lower quarters were put on the surgical schedule. Pesky, hard-to-maintain walls in the living/dining room were covered with more of that carefree, durable paneling. We laid wall-to-wall carpeting there and in the kitchen, improving the aesthetic as well as the physical value of rooms nipped by Minnesota's head-on confrontation with Old Man Winter.

A year later, the anemic and neglected screened porch underwent treatment. Previously unable to contribute anything other than dust and spiders to the family's livelihood, thanks to more—you guessed it—paneling, it became a combination guest room, mini-library, and reading room that now houses our organ.

In 1974, plastic surgery was prescribed for the kitchen's brittle, splintering countertops. After careful prepping, a tailor-made but preassembled Formica work surface was installed to choruses of "Thank you . . . thank you."

Meanwhile, that little bathroom's only claim to distinction was its identity as a small, dingy space rather than a large one. So several half-days of labor transformed the chronically crumbling and flaking plaster walls into satiny plastic, washable ones.

Most recently, after our teenage boys threatened to cease and desist at choretime unless we did something about the dank and drear of their bedroom, we did something about their bedroom.

That understanding landlord called in a master of the miter box who, in less than three days, turned their second-story dungeon into Kings' Castle with—what else?—wood paneling (manly western pine this time). And I was blessed with a dividend in the deal, because the room's long, awkward closet was split into two— one a walk-in for the boys and the other for general storage, with access from the adjacent hallway. Praises to the Lord, again, for small favors.

The most critical and prolonged operation—yet the easiest—took place in my seven by nine feet workroom adjoining the kitchen. A series of minor implants turned four flat walls into a room that can handle laundry, sewing, record keeping, and writing activities. Nothing fancy—and minimal in cost—but the results are crucial to the organization of the whole household.

Hung above the washer and dryer is a simple cupboard with flexible shelving that holds laundry supplies and ironing and pressing equipment. On a second wall, above my plywood-over-file-cabinet desk, is a larger but similar cupboard that accommodates paper supplies, greeting cards, glue, tape, and miscellaneous items needed for correspondence and record keeping.

Stationed on a third wall is the sewing center, still in need of refinement and beyond description at this point, but serving the important purpose of keeping sewing and mending supplies together around the sewing machine.

For this rehabilitating history and to the Lord who led us here in the beginning, I am thankful. To Honeymoon House, just for being and for standing still for our progeny and patchwork, I am grateful.

WHEN IN DOUBT, MOVE IT OUT

"Ain't I a good stacker and piler-upper, Lord?"

"That you are," He replied. "Now if you were just a better sorter and thrower-awayer, you'd be in business."

"No argument from this corner," I said, "but all those decisions! What to keep for the great-grand-children, what to toss into the Hefty bag. . . ."

"True, it's a brain-draining job," He said, "but unless you want to build on about six more rooms by the time you're fifty, you need a better saving system. Elimination is an important part of organization, in more ways than one."

"You're in charge," I acknowledged. "What do You recommend? For instance, about throwing things away—some times it's so easy, other times as hopeless as finding the cap for the family-size toothpaste."

"Well, how often do you get the urge to fill the trash barrel?"

"Hmmm . . ." came my ready response, "uh . . . well, now that you've asked, I immediately realize it's about once a month—just before my menstrual period, in fact."

"Good thinking! That's your nesting instinct coming through. At that time the hormone balance in your body is similar to just before childbirth, when you're certainly being prepared for 'nesting.' It makes you more interested in the fine points of homemaking than you are at other times."

"Aha!" I whooped. "So if I'd *plan* to do my sorting and discarding jobs at that time of the month. . . ."

"Right!" He applauded. "Use those few days—it could be as long as a week—to clean drawers, tidy closets, sort hand-me-downs. Write those letters you've been putting aside, balance your checkbook, pay bills. . . ."

"Sounds reasonable, but that would still leave me with one of the major occupational hazards of house-wifery."

"And what's that?"

"Oh, You know."

"Yes, but tell Me anyway," He insisted.

"Well, judging from what I hear on the party line, we all seem to run into the same problem. We save things for years, but never need them until about three hours after they've been buried in the sanitary land-fill."

"There's a time to keep and a time to throw away" (Eccl. 3:6), He said. "What you need is a halfway house. Take those gadgets and gizmos that are cluttering your drawers, that old gooseneck lamp that's just taking up space in the hall closet, and those boxes of Carter's that really didn't wear out before the kids grew up. Relegate them to a high shelf or to your attic. Get them out of your most usable storage space. Then after a year or so, if you haven't used them or found someone who can, or if they won't even go at the corner rummage sale or at a thrift shop, feel free to set them out for the sanitation engineers. And incidentally," He whispered, "I'm not above helping you make those decisions."

"I'll take You up on that offer in a couple of weeks," I promised.

"In the meantime, you could bear in mind that the Father and I sent you the Holy Spirit to help you in all your weaknesses, whatever your weaknesses may be," He added.

"When did You do that?" I asked.

"When you decided to let go and let God," He answered.

"So that's what happened!"

"Right. So just ask for a fresh portion of the Helper every morning, at least, and He'll be right there. Believe it or not, I can tell a a good magazine from one that's ready for the pulp shredder."

"Will You forgive me if I throw out my recipe for Jamaican Rabbit Eclairs?" I asked.

"Does Julia Child wear an apron?"

SHELVE IT

I stumbled into the office of the local lumberyard, impaled myself on the invoice spindle, and cried, "Please, *please*. Cut me a couple of slabs of extra-thick plywood, twenty by fifty-two inches. And if it isn't too much trouble, I need some one-by-tens too."

"I'll see what I can do," said Larry the Logger.

"What are you working on today? A bomb shelter?"

"Close. It's for my workroom."

A stop at the hardware store for adjustable shelf stripping gave me everything I needed to complete my undercover project. *Almost* everything. I was counting on some spousely sympathy to volunteer for the hammer-and-screwdriver detail.

It worked. My brainstorm brought me much-needed bookshelves for my one-wall "library" and shelving and workspace that have made my workroom really workable instead of just a panorama of frustrating jumble—or was it jumbled frustration?

EVERYTHING IN ITS PLACE

Secretaries have file cabinets. Doctors have file cabinets. Farmers have file cabinets. Why shouldn't housewifery be entitled to a few manila folders, too?

"Now you're thinking!" It was my Counselor again. "I've been waiting for you to realize that. You've been doing a better job sorting things, and you're just a step away from the ultimate in orderliness."

I was ready for my first file cabinet. I went for a four-drawer model—and filled it easily. Letters, report cards, snapshots waiting for an album, bills, vacation ideas, addresses, sheet music, appliance warranties, gift wrap—the possibilities seemed as prolific as my imagination. I was glad I didn't buy the cheapest model available—those things need to be able to hold a lot of weight and take a lot of pushing and pulling.

"I think I've got it made," I cheered. "Thanks for the tip, Lord."

It took me some time and a gross of file folders to get everything in its place, but I consulted the Lord in the process, and for me it's paying better dividends than Merrill Lynch, Pierce, Fenner, or Smith.

OUTLINE FOR A HOME FILING SYSTEM

A. Home accounts
   1. Bills unpaid
   2. Bills paid
   3. Canceled checks, bank statements
   4. Receipts, deposit slips
   5. Recordbooks
B. Personal correspondence
   1. Addresses
   2. Letters to be answered
   3. Birthdays
   4. Gift ideas
   5. Sheets of gift wrap
C. Family Living
   1. Education (report cards, college catalogs, etc.)
   2. Vacations
   3. Family Night ideas
D. Clothing
   1. Planning
   2. Patterns
E. Food
   1. Menus and new recipes
   2. Menus for special occasions
F. Furnishings

G. Appliances (warranties and operating instructions)
H. Lawn and garden
I. Home structure (building and remodeling ideas)
J. Organizations
   1. Church
   2. Community
   3. Youth
K. Miscellaneous

MY SECRET DREAMS

"Lord, You said we have not because we ask not. So I'm asking: If You should see fit to disrupt Honeymoon House just one more time, there are a few miscellanies I'd like to have.

"When we really get down to basics, the truth is I have a passion for kitchen doors, specifically kitchen doors that can be closed when I deem it necessary. I love cooking for a crowd. But when it comes to cooking *in* a crowd—I'm sorry—I'm an ugly spoilsport.

"On those doors I'd like to have neon billboards carrying messages such as:

We'll call you when we have an opening.

or

Search warrant required for admission.

or

*This evening's entree will be Sweet and Sour Pork,
prepared by a cook who is likewise.*

"And I'd like to have my kitchen windows facing the early morning sun to help me get started in the morning. I realize this could complicate things, being the kitchen is located on the northwest corner of the house. In lieu of that, then, I'd be grateful for a family room that the kids could sort of consider their territory, leaving the living room as quieter space for a "big people" hospitality room when needed.

"And just one more little thing. I don't like to appear unappreciative, but we *really* could use another bathroom, a half bath at least. It would be so nice to be able to use the little room as long as necessary without holding up a parade.

"Still, if none of these is in my future, I don't mind. I know 'I've got a mansion, just over the hilltop.' "

chapter 6.

WE'RE IN THIS MESS TOGETHER

Every manager worth his checklist writes an occasional memo. I paper the house with them.

To encourage family cooperation when the top of the refrigerator became an untidy repository for assorted keepsakes, this reminder (in my handwriting) appeared atop the Frigidaire:

> This is NOT Treasure Island.
> Please find a more appropriate
> place for your valuables.

When curious and/or idle hands too regularly disturbed my combination office/sewing/laundry room, I posted this one on the door:

YOUR GRACIOUS ATTENTION, PLEASE!

The little woman who makes the cubicle behind this door her home within a home begs your mercy in helping her maintain some sense of order, and consequently her sanity, in this area.

Please stay out if at all possible. If necessary to enter, please do so quickly, quietly, and without leaving any disturbing evidence of your presence. Many thanks.

P.S. If you have a roommate who cannot yet read, please pass the word.

To help banish washday blues, I issued this epistle:

Dear Family:

The Laundry Staff of our household has informed me there will be no more room-to-room pickup service on washday. Only items deposited in hampers will be laundered.

The laundry workers also stated they feel each person should learn to take some responsiblity for his/her own clothes and thereby decrease Washday Drudgery by doing the following before putting clothes into hampers:

1. Empty all pockets.
2. Close zippers.
3. Turn all clothing, except corduroy, *right* side out. If corduroy, turn *wrong* side out.

WE'RE IN THIS MESS TOGETHER

4. Clip matching socks together with clothespins.
Only clothing prepared as instructed above will be washed.

Love, Mom

In a subsequently successful attempt to encourage cheerful and willing hearts for family devotions, this written announcement became a supper table centerpiece:

There will be a short inspirational (we hope) session in the living room immediately following supper. Please bring your Bible and a willing spirit.

To discourage wasting time through boob tube addiction, the top of the television set became a billboard for this admittedly unoriginal message:

"... whatever things are true, whatever things are noble, whatever things are just, whatever things are pure, whatever things are lovely, whatever things are of good report, if there is any virtue and if there is anything praiseworthy—meditate on these things."

—Phil. 4:8

Permanently installed in our side entry is another memo, not from me but from a Roman Catholic nun.

Her watercolor painting, which I purchased in a hospital lounge where she displayed her work, is titled:

Relax. God loves you.

That one covers all the others.

MYSTERIES AND MAXIMS

Eighteen years into motherhood and I still have no sure answers to:

- How to make a preschooler's enthusiasm for household chores come alive again at thirteen.
- How to explain to adolescent ears—regarding housekeeping standards—the difference between "casual" and "casualty."
- How the mailman can deliver trash faster than the junk man can remove it.
- Why I can have a neat assortment of twenty-seven pens and sharpened pencils one day and none the next.
- Why it's apparently easier to remove one's shoes and socks in the middle of a living room than in one's own bedroom.
- How someone named Not Me can seemingly occupy so much time spilling, breaking, and "borrowing" things without ever being seen by the human eye.

On the other hand, experience has given me a few workable theorems for provoking family cooperation in maintaining some order in a household.

- Unless you head a household of soldiers, don't ask your family to follow army rules. Hopefully, they won't bc called into battle without more specific preparation.
- Try to keep regular times for certain chores to be done. Those who must help with meals, for example, are more likely to remember and cooperate if mealtimes are regular.
- An automatic dishwasher is not a luxury. It's a health helper, a frustration fighter, and a very effective way to free time for more lasting activities.
- Provide sufficient pegs and shelves for children's belongings at heights that are easy for them to reach.
- Don't *send* a child to do a job that is new to him. Be ready and willing to take the time to do it *with* him at first and stand willing to help occasionally, even as he becomes more capable and responsible.
- Set aside a few drawers or cubbyholes for miscellaneous throw-ins or a "lost and found" department.
- If careless clutter is a problem, establish a "Boo-Boo Box." Use it for temporary storage of clothing and other personal items that have not been put away at the end of a day. Don't allow anyone—including Mom and Dad—to retrieve anything until the end of the week. If you wish, specify a certain penalty that can be paid if a confiscated item is crucial for life support.
- Relax and keep a sense of humor. Remember, in "keeping house" together, the rewards of the togetherness are far more numerous and longer lasting than those of the housekeeping.

AN END TO THE PAPER CHASE

"Oh, no! Baby unrolled the toilet paper again!" I moaned.

Ann Landers thought *she* had problems. One of her readers raised the question: Which is the correct way to put toilet paper on the dispenser—up the back and down the front, or up the front and down the back? Thenceforth, she received so much bipartisan mail from her readers that she finally had to stand on her chair and cry, "No more! Please!"

At our house it took us five full infancies to answer the same question—but we settled it with more finality than Ann did.

For more than thirty years, including six as a mother of toddlers in various stages of toddling, I was an up the back and down the frontist on the toilet paper hanging issue. It rolls off more easily that way, especially in the black of night when you've opted for leaving the lights off and aren't too sure where the roll is, let alone its end. As a result, I suffered through much rerolling, never earning as much as a B-minus for neatness.

One day, apparently fearing that this phenomenon alone would wipe out any potential I had for sainthood, my husband decided to study the situation. He coaxed the youngest into the bathroom, stood him in front of the paper dispenser. "See the nice paper? Touch the pretty paper," he tempted. Cherubic cooperation provided the answer Dad was looking for.

"They haven't been pulling the paper off," Hubby explained. "They've been *patting* it off, a natural activity for those little creatures. One pat gets the thing started cascading to the floor—just the beginning of a fascinating game. But when the paper goes up the front and down the back, patting from above doesn't produce a thing."

The head of the family claims this as his biggest contribution to housewifery's enlightenment. As far as I'm concerned, that one was worth a dozen other wife savers.

"Lord, you had to go over my head with that one," I said after the episode, "but thanks, anyway. Little things mean a lot."

THIS, TOO . . .

Diaper changing became so routine and automatic that I couldn't remember doing the last one.

And the Lord said, "This, too, shall pass."

Brothers, surrounded by a yard full of toys, fought over a battered tennis ball.

And the Lord said, "This, too, shall pass."

Sleepless nights during flu season were followed by long, headachey days.

And the Lord said, "This, too, shall pass."

Little hands reached into the cookie jar for "Just one more?"

And the Lord said, "This, too, shall pass."

We didn't go to "buck nite" at the drive-in movie because of insufficient funds.

And the Lord said, "This, too, shall pass."

I stiffened in the passenger seat while my student driver first-born practiced her left turns.

And the Lord said, "This, too, shall pass."

We sat elbow-to-elbow around the supper table, everyone talking at once.

And the Lord said, "This, too, shall pass."

The afternoon schoolbus dispersed a half-dozen chattering Kramers, and from the first one through the door I heard, "I got a hundred in spelling today, Mom!"

And the Lord said, "This, too, shall pass."

My husband and I came home to a quiet house after an evening out and peeked in on our offspring, sleeping peacefully in their beds.

And the Lord said, "This, too, shall pass."

PUTTING THE FAMILY FIRST

"Where are you going, Mom?" asked the four-year-old dumpling at the bathroom door.

"Nowhere," I replied.

"Then why do you smell so good?" she asked again.

What smelled so good to her was only shower soap and my routine facial moisturizer, and I thought to myself, "How wise you are, little one, but how sad that you've already learned to associate good with going."

I was reminded of a poem that a visitor in our home scribbled on my kitchen memo pad in our early "before children" days. He wrote:

We have careful words for the stranger
    and smiles for the one-time guest
But oft for our own the bitter tone
    Though we love our own the best.

Don't we all tend to save our best for "going somewhere," for people outside our homes? I asked. We wear our best clothes, comb our hair more carefully, and exercise our most courteous manners for people who might not even miss us if we were to disappear from the earth tomorrow. The ones we love best often stand at the end of the line for our time, as well as for our kindest words and best appearances. "God setteth the solitary in families . . . ," but we become so busy running in one direction and another for assorted meetings and programs, that an evening with an entire family—even a very small family—together at home is more accidental than customary.

And the Lord said, "It doesn't need to be that way. Fighting the touch-and-go rat race is a tough battle for a family, but it's worth the fight."

Here's my battle plan for getting my group together:

- Make home such a nice place to be that it will at least occasionally compare favorably with something outside.
- Find the "off" button on the TV.
- A bowl of hot buttered popcorn, a game of Risk, even school homework, can be points of interest for relaxed evenings together as a family.
- Be there when really needed by friends, relatives, church, or community. But remember, "Home is the best place to be."

Try these recipes for at-home family evenings:

OVEN CARAMEL CORN

18 cups of popped popcorn
2 cups brown sugar

PEANUT BUTTER ON MY PILLOW

1 cup butter or margarine
½ cup light corn syrup
1 pinch of salt
½ teaspoon soda
1 cup of nuts, if desired.

Mix sugar, butter, syrup and salt and boil over medium heat for 5 minutes. Add soda and mix well. Pour over corn; stir until corn is coated fairly evenly. Spread on cookie sheets and bake for 1 hour at 200-225 degrees F., stirring every fifteen minutes. Spread on clean countertop to cool, breaking to separate as it cools.

POPCORN CRUNCH

½ cup melted butter
½ cup honey
3 quarts of popped popcorn
1 cup nuts.

Mix butter and honey. Heat until well blended. Pour over popcorn and nuts. Mix well. Spread in thin layer on a cookie sheet. Bake at 350 degrees F. for 10-15 minutes. Cool and separate.

chapter 7.

QUIET! PLEASE!

"Mother! Why are you wearing the stereo head-phones in the kitchen?"

"Can't hear you, dear. I'm wearing the stereo headphones."

"How can you hear anything on them with no cord and this far from the stereo?"

"You're probably wondering how I can get anything on them away from the stereo. Actually, I've got them plugged into my pacemaker."

The last time I checked, tooth decay was considered the most common disease in this country—perhaps in the world. But I contend there's another malady equal to it: Decibel Disease.

Load the dishwasher, flip a harmless-looking little

switch, and koochunka! I've invited seventy-five decibels of frothing, churning, choking action into what is supposed to be a harbor for weary souls—our humble home. Comes time to mow the lawn, and the week's mower-designate pulls a machine from the garage and circles the yard with ninety decibels of rotorblades. He finishes the job, and we discover a neighbor riding ninety-five decibels of the same with a half acre to go.

Back in the house, sixty decibels of canned guffaws spew from the Chromacolor theater, perhaps the undisputed champion of Decibel Disease infection. Even such seemingly silent sentries as the refrigerator and the freezer cyclically send forty or more decibels into their surroundings. The clothes dryer rolls merrily along at fifty-five decibels, and stereo makers have had the audacity to build as much as 120 decibels into their products. (Thankfully, we've never put that one to the test, but I cower in the knowledge that it's within the realm of possibility.)

No, I've never actually used headphones to blot out any of these aural assaults, even in a dentist's chair, but I've been tempted.

EARS TUNED TO PARADISE, NOT PANDEMONIUM

Noise hurts. It's one of the stresses I wrote about in Chapter 4. Many scientists agree that a continual noise level averaging as low as seventy dB can damage hearing. Our bodies, ears included, were designed for the tranquillity and ease of Eden—not the hammering, harangues, and jet power of the twentieth century. Although we're usually not aware of it, each of us makes a specific physiological adjustment every time his eardrums vibrate.

"Loud noises once in a while probably cause no harm," says Dr. Gerd Jansen of Ruhr University. "But chronic noise situations must be pathological. Constant exposure to noise is negative to your health."*

A speeding truck whooshes past the front door, and it seems that every hair on my body rises to meet the challenge. Thunder claps overhead in the night and my heart, I'm sure, skips a beat. An accumulation of kitchen noises stimulates an instinct to flee to a tropical forest.

And speaking of kitchens, if yours is like mine, on an average day it's probably the noisiest room in the house. I understand that back in the prehistoric days when all kitchen work was done with elbow grease and a butcher knife, it was a quieter place. All of that changed with the arrival of garbage disposals, blenders, and exhaust fans in a room that usually has a high percentage of hard surfaces that reflect sound rather than absorbing it.

Government agencies get their share of criticism, but one that has done some work that housewifery could be thankful for is the Environmental Protection Agency (EPA). They've done some sound thinking, and here are some of their guidelines about noise control techniques in planning a kitchen:

(1) Choose a floor plan which locates the

*"Noise: A Health Problem," Office of Noise Abatement and Control, Environmental Protection Agency, Washington, D.C. 20460.

kitchen as far as possible from such noise-sensitive areas as bedrooms, studies, or formal living rooms.

(2) Design the kitchen as a completely enclosed, sound-insulated room.

(3) Select "quiet" appliances, and insist on proper vibration-isolated mounting or installation. (Products are now supposed to be labeled according to how much noise they make, thanks to the Noise Control Act of 1972.)

(4) Install sound-absorbing materials on room surfaces to reduce the noise buildup due to excessive reverberation. Materials, such as acoustical ceiling tile, draperies and curtains, carpets or throw rugs, and even ranks of exposed towelling, can provide a considerable reduction in kitchen noise level.

Anyone who is "installed" in a kitchen where points(1) and (2) are history can still use points (3) and (4) to advantage. Here's an EPA drawing that gives some fairly simple and inexpensive adjustments that can be made to cut your chances of contracting the Decibel Disease in your own kitchen.

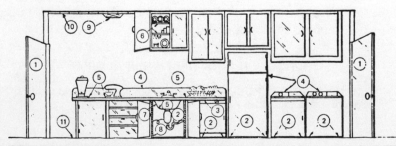

(1) Install solid door with gaskets

(2) Use vibration isolators & mounts

(3) Isolate appliance from cabinet with rubber gasket

(4) Insert rubber gaskets behind cabinets and appliances to avoid wall contact

(5) Place rubber pads under small units, dish racks and in sink basins

(6) Install rubber or cork tile on backs and shelves of cabinets

(7) Apply vibration damping material

(8) Install acoustic tile

(9) Install exhaust fan on rubber mounts

(10) Install acoustic ceiling

(11) Install carpet or foam backed tile

LIVING THE QUIET LIFE

Difficult as it may be to come by, I thrive on peace and quiet. Show me anybody who doesn't, and I'll show you a disco club.

Considering the world's noise pollution and where and how it all started, I suspected that the Lord might be sporting earplugs, too. So I went to His Word and asked, "What do You think of the din we're in?"

In First Thessalonians 4:11, He said: ". . . aspire to lead a quiet life. . . ."

In Proverb 17:1, He told me, "Better a dry crust with peace and quiet than a house full of feasting, with strife."

Another Proverb, 9:13, said, "The woman Folly is loud; she is undisciplined and without knowledge." In Ecclesiastes 6:11 He gave me something more that that woman Folly, whoever she is, could take to heart: "The more the words, the less the meaning, and how does that profit anyone?"

He seemed to sum it up in Psalm 46:10 where He says, *"Be still,* and know that I am God . . ." (italics mine).

While much can be done about noise in and around the home, I know from maddening experience that there's still much of it that we have to live with. Some of the buffering has to come from inside—from a heart filled with peace and quiet that only Jesus can provide. As Isaiah said, "The fruit of righteousness will be peace; the effect of righteousness will be quietness and confidence forever" (Isa. 32:17).

HOW TO DETERMINE YOUR GOING-BANANAS PROBABILITY FACTOR

Here's a self-test device to determine if you are in any grave danger of flipping out over excessive noise.

Part A

If you live within one hundred yards of a
freeway, give yourself ten bananas. _____

If your family car has a washing machine
engine, you get five bananas. _____

Give yourself one banana for each child in
your family. _____

For each child who is "verbally prolific,"
add another banana. _____

If the underside of an airborne 747 at close
range is a common sight in your neighborhood, collect a bunch of ten. _____

If you have a child who plays drums in the
school band and must practice at home,
score three bananas. _____

For each television set in your household,
claim five bananas. _____

102

If you live next door to a kennel or its
equivalent, score three bananas. _____

If you are regularly in prolonged contact
with any adult who claims to be a true
intellectual and has "serious concerns
of conscience, which *must* be voiced,"
grab five more bananas. _____

TOTAL ══════

Part B

If the walls of your house have sound
proofing insulation, return ten bananas. _____

If your neighborhood employs a goat herd
to mow lawns, give five bananas to the
herd. _____

If your doors are solid-core rather than
hollow, hand back at least three
bananas. _____

If your telephone is a desk-model rather
than wall-mounted, deduct one banana. _____

If you appreciate FM-radio more than
AM, subtract three more bananas. _____

If your home is at least seventy-five percent carpeted, give up five bananas. _____

If most of your windows have draperies or
generous curtaining, subtract five. _____

For each room with an acoustical tile ceiling, subtract one banana. _____

BALANCE ══════

INTERMISSION

If you live alone in central Antarctica, invite a New Yorker down for the weekend.

If you're legally deaf, disregard Parts A and B.

If you're not deaf but occasionally wish you were, count your blessings. Now go on to Part C.

Part C: Solutions

What was that?! Where's your noise coming from? For homes with air conditioners (room or window):

☐ Adjust thermostat to minimize starting and stopping.

☐ Install gasket between unit and wall or window.

☐ Clean filters weekly to prevent clogging and subsequent whistling noise.

If you are considering a food blender:

☐ Select model with glass rather than plastic container.

☐ Select model with low-noise rating.

To cope with children's voices and play noises:

☐ Use sound-absorbent materials in playrooms.

☐ Treat ventilation ducts with sound-absorbing lining.

In dealing with your alarm clock:

☐ Choose a chiming alarm or a wake-to-music radio alarm.

☐ Place the clock on a soft padded surface.

Regarding your clothes washer and dryer:
- ☐ Use sound-absorbing materials in laundry area.
- ☐ Install appliances on resilient pads.
- ☐ Isolate laundry area from other living space as much as possible.

For cabinet doors:
- ☐ Tighten loose strike plates.
- ☐ Choose solid-core, well-damped doors.

If you own or plan to buy a dishwasher:
- ☐ Install flexible connectors in pipe and drain lines to minimize vibration conduction.
- ☐ Mount unit on resilient pads and isolate from enclosure with rubber gaskets.
- ☐ Ask for a comparative demonstration to determine noise level before buying.

For your heating system:
- ☐ Lower thermostat at night.
- ☐ Use resilient mounts under the motor/blower, resilient hangers, flexible boots, and acoustic lining in ducts.
- ☐ Air flow systems with simple layouts are quieter than complex layouts.

For staircases to the basement or second floor:
- ☐ Carpeting or resilient pads on the treads.
- ☐ Fireproof, sound-absorbing material on the upper walls.

And, finally, the telephone:
- ☐ Select desk-type model rather than wall-mounted.
- ☐ Select model with volume control.
- ☐ Place phone on a soft rubber pad.

For More Information:

Noise: A Health Problem—A pamphlet that discusses the various harmful effects of noise in and around the home.

Quieting in the Home—A manual of practical and detailed ideas for subduing noise in the home.

You can get either or both free of charge by writing: Office of Noise Abatement and Control, Environmental Protection Agency (AW-471) Washington, D.C. 20460

chapter 8.

DIVERSIONARY TACTICS

It was January, 1978. Eleven-day excursions to mainland China were in heavy demand—at $2200 per head. Plane tickets to Denver and to Colorado's ski resorts were hard to come by in some areas, as the snow-covered slopes made up for the previous winter's poor conditions. Vacation trips to South America were selling as never before.

The Kramer clan had neither the inclination, the greenbacks, nor the energy for any of these. That was the year we discovered that for a lot less money and minimal effort, a family can "hole up" in a full-facility motel and have just as much (well, almost as much) fun.

A brief phone call to a suburban Minneapolis motel

was all it took to arrange two adjacent rooms for a bargain-priced family weekend. Then from Friday afternoon through Sunday we had a ball doing nothing, going nowhere. For less than twenty-five dollars per person (food included), we had the most relaxing respite in our history up to that time.

Conditions for making the trip included a few bendable rules:

1. Don't pack clothing or other essentials in grocery bags. It takes the romance out of the trip. (Guess what mother was seen sneaking up a side stairway at the Holiday Inn clutching a rumpled brown bag containing a half-used tube of Crest, a pair of tennis shoes, (size 1½), thirteen hair curlers, a needle and spool of thread, and an extra set of clothes for the three-year-old?)

2. Be careful. Remember that the contents of a heated pool can drown one as effectively as ice-water lakes and streams. (If this suggestion was kept in mind by the splashing younger set, it was not obvious to their parents, who regularly went into cardiac arrest at poolside.)

3. Total volume of purchases at the nearby discount store cannot exceed the body capacity of one Chevrolet Kingswood station wagon when also occupied by ten persons known to object to cramped quarters. (The area U-Haul agency was notified to stand by. However, careful logistics determined that a Fuzzy Pumper Barber Shop and a Vertibird Airborne Rescue Mission could be wedged between the driver and the steering wheel provided he/she temporarily refrained from breathing.)

4. Limit trips to any and all pop machines, espe-

cially after six P.M. (As expected, the teenagers of the entourage easily circumvented this one with purchase of no-deposit, no-return bottles at the above-mentioned discount store.)

5. Feel free to sleep late and/or don't disturb your parents at least until sunrise. Because your father is footing the bill, he would like to be able to think of this as his vacation as well. (Score: 1 win, 1 loss. Saturday began with the hiss of the channel five color pattern, *Roadrunner,* the *Pink Panther* and, at 7:45 A.M., the first of countless elevator trips to the pool. Sunday rising time was more agreeable to the generative elders, thanks to the exhaustion incurred the previous day.)

6. Eat whatever, whenever, and wherever you wish, bearing in mind that this privilege will be totally abolished upon returning home, where your mother, the cook, looks with disfavor upon short-order meals, room service, and candy snacks. (Full cooperation. Products of Hershey, Hostess, and Reese's marketing genius were kept in good supply in our rooms at all times and, seriously speaking, a large part of the delight found in the vacation was the fact that the family cook was off duty and restaurant orders were restricted only by the available menus. Frequent repeats were heartily recommended by all.)

Lord, we thank you for our Nothing Times. We need these times to re-create ourselves, to help renew our spirits for the busy times. We thank you for stopping the world so we can get off once in a while. . . .

CALL AHEAD

A telephone is probably the best tool for getting information on weekend family plans at specific motels or hotels. Here are the toll-free numbers of many of the country's chains. If the toll-free operator doesn't have family-plan rates for a specific franchise in your area, she can supply its phone number so you can call the facility directly.

Best Western	1-800-528-1234
Canadian Pacific Reserve-A-Room	1-800-828-7447
Days Inns	1-800-241-2345
Downtowner-Roundtowner	1-800-238-6161
Holiday Inn	1-800-238-8000
Hospitality Inns	1-800-321-2323
Howard Johnson's	1-800-654-2000
Hyatt House	1-800-228-9000
Marriott	1-800-228-9290
Master Hosts	1-800-238-6040
Quality Inns	1-800-228-5151
Ramada Inn	1-800-228-2828
Red Carpet Inns	1-800-231-3648
Rodeway Inns	1-800-228-2000
Sheraton	1-800-325-3535
Radisson	1-800-228-9822
Superior Motels	1-800-241-1322
Travelodge	1-800-255-3050
Royal Inns	1-800-854-2933
Utell International	1-800-621-1015

HONEYMOON REFRESHERS

No offense, kids, but there come times when—if we

know what's good for us—Mom and Dad need to get away together. Mind you, we don't do it "to get away from the kids." We just want to be together—alone.

For future reference, for the day you're in our shoes, here's how, as an old bride (or groom), you can tell when it's time for another honeymoon:

When the stars in your eyes begin turning to barbs on your tongue.

When you're Cometing the bathroom sink and you ask of the mirror, "Now what do *you* want?"

When you go to a wedding and catch yourself thinking, "Fools . . . fools . . ."

When you get your hair done and *nobody* notices.

When you're sure you've got mountains that Mohammed couldn't subdue.

When you know you can't stand to hear, "Oh, didn't I tell you?" one more time.

Brief though it may need to be, a second (third, fourth, fifth . . .) honeymoon can keep you out of the frying pan—*and* out of the divorce courts.

But don't go too far away. It takes too long to get home again.

THE ULTIMATE ENERGIZER

Diversions are priceless; they can determine the life or death of a family. "Authorities" recommend that parents go out alone—together—one night a week and take a weekend vacation once a month. (In defense of and fairness to children, I recommend a family week-end mini-vacation at least three or four times a year.)

But between and within—over, under, and

throughout—these getaways waits a diversion with more lasting rejuvenating power than candlelight dinners and whirlpool saunas. It's the power from on high, invisible, invincible, the only complete energizer—the power of God's Holy Spirit. We need only believe and ask.

MY MUSICAL RESPITE

Oh, what a relief it was! Managing to get to my community band's practice session one Thursday evening after too long an absence, I came away with a new appreciation for the group.

For four years after the band's formation in 1969 I had watched silently and enviously as the all-male aggregation blew their own horns. When the men decided they needed some musical helpmates and voted to admit women to membership, I pulled my moldy saxophone from beneath the bed, beat the path to their practice room door, and continued to do so each week until other obligations kept me from attending more than a few practices and concerts.

The return was a welcome refreshment. That weekly "therapy" session helps me use the remainder of the week to better advantage—I'm a better wife, mother, and household manager because of it. Problems appear in better perspective after an evening of Karl King marches, Broadway show tunes, rambling overtures, and pop tunes of bygone years. The combination of mental concentration and the simple, yet invigorating exercise of controlled breathing and blowing clears my head, both mentally and physically.

Would that everyone could have such a delightful diversion!

By the way, the Chatfield Brass Band, through its Free Music-Lending Library, stands ready, willing, and eager to assist any group or community interested in performing instrumental music.

A loan of any of its 27,000 compositions is available free of charge from:

> Chatfield Brass Band
> Free Music–Lending Library
> Chatfield, Minnesota 55923

Titles of numbers wanted and instrumentation needed must be specified.

BUILDING A MUSICAL FOUNDATION

The diversionary and recreational advantages of a musical adulthood come most easily after some years of juvenile preparation, a task not always appreciated before the age of twenty.

The first time I talked by phone with the lady who was to become a virtual family member via all the piano lessons she fed into some of our offspring, I was impressed by her voice. I pictured a thirty-five-year-old redhead with a svelte 120-pound figure, dressed in the latest styles from Le Coutouriere. (Oh, those stereotypes!)

What I heard was *not* what we got. Jewell Shannon is a grey-haired grandmother, a Methodist minister's wife, a mother of six children, the kind of person you expect to hug you and kiss you and pass you her cookie jar—and sometimes she does.

But she's a piano teacher par excellence! And these are some of the values she sees in musical education:

- A means of expressing emotions, of letting off steam.
- A means of developing emotional sensitivity to others' feelings.
- Self-discipline, from the necessity of a regular beat and regular and repetitive practice.
- Appreciation of beauty.
- Development of the memory.
- Self-confidence.
- A means of becoming a good listener, musically.

BE POSITIVE ABOUT PRACTICE

Mrs. Shannon knows from much experience how we parents sometimes can undermine our children's accomplishments right from the start. She says that many parents limit what a child may accomplish in piano from the very first lesson, by saying things like:

- *"I don't expect my child to become a concert pianist."* Are you going to make it impossible for him even if he is especially gifted and talented? Why not leave the option open?
- *"I always hated to play scales. . . ."* Say it once, and your child will feel the same way.
- *"We always had to fight with the other kids to get*

them to practice," or *"Should I force my child to practice?"* Do you have to force your child to go to bed, eat proper food, go to school, etc.? This is a parent-child relationship problem, not a musical problem. Say these things once in front of the child, and you *have* a problem.

- *"I don't think a boy will stick with it very long."* Again, *you're* setting the child's attitude— negatively. What about Mozart, Beethoven, Liszt, and Horowitz to name a few? A child will *be* and *do* what you expect of him.

From my own experience—having been witness and party to a decade of not only piano practices, but of trumpet trials, trombone tribulations, saxophone stammers, guitar gyrations, and little zingy zylophones—I'd throw these suggestions in with Mrs. Shannon's advice:

- Be interested, but don't hover.
- Just *expect* that he/she will practice. A positive mental attitude on the part of a parent seems, as if by mental telepathy, to stimulate the child's desire to practice.
- If you play a musical instrument yourself, you've already gone the first mile in getting and keeping your child interested in music and in helping him/her use music as a personal resource later in life.

chapter 9.

LIVING EFFECTIVELY
BETWEEN GOD
AND MAMMON

Money can't buy happiness. True, but it does come in handy in the grocery store, at the gas pumps, and in the dentist's office. Basic things like stereos and vacations and permanent waves, not to mention the little extras—food, clothes, rent payments, safety pins, soap, pencils and paper, lawn mowers—all seem to come most easily in exchange for some of the green stuff.

I have on occasion reflected on the question: "If I had only twenty dollars left—the last I'd ever have—and only my own needs to be concerned about, how would I spend it?"

I always seem to come up with a qualified answer: "It depends on the season of the year and whether I'm in Minnesota at the time. If it's both winter and Minnesota, I'd blow it on heating oil or long underwear or another sweater—whatever it would take to keep me mobile a little longer. I'd be counting on my ability to find something deep in the carpet pile to pacify my stomach. Otherwise, if it were spring, summer, or fall, I'd probably go for food."

Then, at the thought of *food*, I come to my senses. Being a partner in the business of farming—working to help feed the world—I'm a little touchy about food prices.

When I hear, "Food is so expensive," I want to scream, "Compared to what?" And sometimes I do.

If I ever get up on my soap box on that subject, I'll be asking some pointed questions:

"How much of your food bill is *food* and how much is built-in cook's service?

"How often do you buy fully cooked foods that you just heat or thaw and serve? That's mostly a cook's service, not food.

"How does what you spend on food compare to what you lay out for your Oldsmobile?

"How much goes up in the smoke of a Pall Mall?

"Disappears at the municipal liquor store?

"In hobby equipment?

"Vacation travel?"

Then, having had my say, I'll grab my grocery cart, call to mind all my smart shopper tips, and thank the Lord for the fabulous selection at my fingertips.

BREAD UPON WATERS

"You know, Rita, I just can't figure it out. You're a

family of ten, but you all seem so healthy and well-fed. You're as well-dressed as most. You've got two cars in the garage, one somewhat newer than the other, but both in operating condition. It just doesn't add up!''

"Probably not—because I don't know what you're talking about, dear friend," I said.

"What I mean is . . . it isn't supposed to work that way. With so many mouths to feed, you're supposed to be *poor*. Your husband's just a farmer—doesn't own even one acre of land. How do you manage without food stamps and holes in your underwear?''

"Be careful how you say 'just a farmer.' But who says we don't have holes in our underwear?'' I laughed.

"Well, that's for you to know, but, well . . . I don't know how to say it except: *How do you do it? I* can't make ends meet, and my family isn't half the size of yours.''

"You mean, how do I balance the budget? Something like that?'' I asked.

"Right. I know it's a nosy question.''

"Not at all. I've nothing to hide. In fact, I'm glad you asked. There's a fantastic story I'd like to share. And many, many others could tell you of similar experiences.''

"Please do.''

"With pleasure. Well, I'll begin by assuring you that it hasn't always been thus. There were the days when I carefully budgeted every dime and still had too much month left at the end of the money—even back when I could easily keep our food costs (for five or six of us at that time) down to twenty dollars a week. Imagine!

Now I could blow that much for one good bedtime snack. And we had medical bills that wouldn't stop, insurance needs that kept increasing, hardly enough money to buy a pair of shoes without juggling the budget . . ."

"It was that rough, huh?" she said soberly.

"Well, no, I didn't think of it as *rough*. I just accepted it as a fact of life for a young, growing family. I knew that when we are faithful over little, we will be given more; as we learn to manage a tight budget well, we become qualified to handle more. But I couldn't envision how that would really happen. It seemed that with the kids still not yet teenagers—people had warned us they'd 'eat us out of house and home' when that time came—things would get worse before they got better."

"Obviously that didn't happen."

"No, and I'll tell you why—and here begins the fantastic part. Things got better just when they *should* have been getting worse because we sort of accidentally plugged in to one of God's promises. After reading a little paperback, *How to Succeed with Your Money* by George Bowman (Moody Press), I was inspired to tithe. It didn't make sense, because it meant doubling what we were giving to our church and to other ministries at the time, and we had to scratch to do that much. But being the family money manager (at my husband's insistence) I asked what he thought about it."

"And he agreed?" my friend asked.

"Well, not exactly. But he didn't veto it either. It

was one of those 'Whatever you think, dear' grunts. So I took the plunge.''

"And?"

"And—well, first let me make one thing perfectly clear: I was led to tithe because of the conviction that *everything* we have *comes* from God, and the *least* we can give Him back is the tithe, ten percent. Furthermore, we pay taxes to the civil government. What about the government of God—doesn't His kingdom deserve our priority support? After all, it *is* a privilege to live within the walk of His city.

"Still, knowing His promises, knowing that he said, *'Give, and it will be given to you: good measure, pressed down, shaken together, and running over . . . For with the same measure that you use, it will be measured back to you'* (Luke 6:38, italics mine), I kept a different kind of financial account those first few months of tithing. . ."

"And?"

"*And* we were thrilled to discover that in those first two or three months, He gave us *back* eight to ten times as much as the amount by which we had increased our giving. That was in *dollars* alone. In addition, there's no way we can know what expenses He may have saved us by keeping us healthy, sparing us from broken windows and clogged carburetors, and so forth. And we really shouldn't have been surprised at all because when we take Him at His Word, believe His promises, stability and prosperity shouldn't come as a surprise.

"So I assume you've stayed with it," she said.

"We wouldn't dare stop!"

"But *how* can you keep it up? Your husband still has the same work, and *you* haven't gone to work."

"I think you may have missed my point—or the principle," I said. "No, I haven't gone to work, nor do I have any plans to. I worked during college, before marriage, as a newlywed, even briefly on a couple of occasions since becoming a mother, but I'm thoroughly convinced that, as long as my husband can provide one full-time income for us, the most 'financially advantageous' place for me is right here at home."

"But you're a writer. Isn't that 'work'?" she asked.

"Well, I suppose so, but not in the usual sense of the word. You see, the Lord has given me the best of all possible worlds: A talent that I can use without leaving my home, and life on a farm where I can help my husband when necessary—but I think of homemaking as my real job. True, doors have begun to open for me as a writer, but the income from it is purely superfluous to our existence."

Pure consternation surfaced on her face.

"Then *where* did those extra dollars come from?" she insisted.

"I've long since forgotten the first ones," I said, "but our biggest step forward—financially—came a couple of years ago when my husband was given the opportunity to buy into the farm on which he had worked ever since we were newlyweds. We took on what some people would consider a rather large 'debt,' but with the Lord's continued help we'll have it paid off in just a handful more years."

"But what if we have another depression—or what if your health fails?"

"If He should, for some reason known only to Him, decide to wither our supply, we'll still trust Him to supply our real *needs* and will keep giving 'as we are prospered.' In the meantime, we're receiving freely and will continue to give freely."

"So you're sold on tithing, I take it."

"Absolutely convinced! When we give with the right attitude—out of a grateful heart and/or a concern to help spread the good news—there's *no way* we can outgive God. Tithing is great. It's critical to successful Christian money management!"

LEARNING TO RECEIVE

"When Christians are living far from God, they find it hard to accept any great blessing from Him, even when He puts it in their laps—but when Christians get close enough to the Lord to feel the true spirit of adoption, they realize how eager He is . . . to pour out good gifts upon His children."

—Hannah Whitall Smith

A SAMPLE BUDGET FORM*

Gross Income $_____
Fixed Expenses
   Income & Payroll Taxes $_____
   Social Security   _____
   Union Dues   _____
   Tithe (10% of Gross)   _____
   Other _____   _____
   _____   _____

Total Fixed Expenses $_____ $_____

Working Income (Deduct Total $_____
     Fixed for Gross Income)

Budgeted %
  $_____Savings
    (10% of Working Income) $_____
  $_____Living Expenses
    (70% of Working Income) $_____

	Monthly	Per Pay Period
Mortgage or Rent	$_____	$_____
Heat	_____	_____
Electricity	_____	_____
Water/Sewage/ Garbage	_____	_____
Telephone	_____	_____
Car Insurance	_____	_____
Gasoline	_____	_____
Car Repairs	_____	_____
Recreation/ Entertainment	_____	_____
Newspapers/ Periodicals	_____	_____
Health Insurance	_____	_____
Life Insurance	_____	_____
Doctors/Medicines	_____	_____
Food/Household	_____	_____
Cleaning/Dry Cleaning	_____	_____
Clothes	_____	_____

*Reprinted by permission from *Your Money Matters* by Malcolm MacGregor, published and copyright 1977, Bethany Fellowship, Inc., Minneapolis, Minnestoa 55438.

Home Furnishings	_____	_____
Emergency	_____	_____
Christmas & Gifts	_____	_____
Vacation	_____	_____
Allowances	_____	_____
Other_____	_____	_____
_____	_____	_____
_____	_____	_____
TOTAL LIVING EXPENSE	$_____	$_____

$_____Debts and Buffer (20% of Working Income)

_____		_____
_____		_____
_____		_____
_____		_____
_____		_____
TOTAL DEBTS	$_____	$_____

HAPPY GIVE AND TAKE

It's more blessed to give than to receive. I believe that. But it has occurred to me that *receiving can be the highest form of giving,* if by receiving we give up our pride, self-sufficiency, and independence to allow God and His human family to serve us in love.

That thought came after experiences of putting my heart into a gift, only to have it driven into the ground by, "Oh, you shouldn't have," or "That's too much," or even, "I can't accept it." In such situations, where is the blessing (happiness) for the giver? I gave a lot of thought to trying to figure why some of the very people who seem so willing to give an arm and a leg to others are the same ones who are most resistant to accepting any kind of giving directed at them.

Then a well-known newspaper columnist gave me a clue. She said that a person who concentrates on giving and doing things for others while resisting gifts or help from others is "selfishness turned inside out." I think she has something there.

And family psychologist Eda LeShan has written in detail of her own experiences in learning to be a gracious receiver. LeShan started thinking about her own one-sided giving habits when a young friend asked her, "Eda, does it always have to be you who does the giving?"

She said, "It has troubled me to realize how often I have refused to allow others the joy of giving because I wanted the pleasure all for myself."

She recalled a time when a friend tried to buy her a new paring knife to replace a defective old one. "I protested so loudly in the store that she was embarrassed and dropped the subject," she wrote. "Now I wish I'd been gracious and had accepted the gift. It was a small thing, but I robbed her of that pleasure. I shall keep my lousy paring knife as a constant reminder!"

She diagnosed her own (and others') overpowering generosity as a subconscious desire to exert power over others, concluding, "It is time for me to become more gracious in allowing others to give to me, to control the impulse to protest."*

Of course, LeShan's wisdom can be carried to the extreme by people who are willing to make givers very happy because they are prepared to do all the taking. A middle ground is perhaps the most blessed territory. Maturity is a balance of generous giving and gracious taking.

*Woman's Day, Dec. 1977.

chapter 10.

WORTH
IT ALL

I had a hard time deciding whether to go to my high
school class reunion. With some of my former classmates getting into cardiac arrest territory, I hated to
have the size of *my* family be the cause of the early
demise of one Eddie Joe Blumhoefer, Class of '55.

At our last reunion, Ed had but three words to say to
me: "*Seven* children? Seven?!" A basketball referee
who calls 'em as he sees 'em, Ed was speechless.

First I thought maybe I could revise my biography.
Instead of *adding* the latest arrival, I considered making a deletion and claiming four of them had wandered
in from the neighbors' and we didn't notice the difference.

No, I'm an honest woman. Naive, perhaps, but honest. Ed's just going to have to face the facts. I think I'll take with me copies of love notes I've composed for my octet. Maybe when he knows the whole story—he'll understand.

Maybe he won't cry, "Foul!" if he reads these.

TO MY FIRST BORN

Dear Kim,

This house became your childhood home on Christmas Day, 1961, when your father brought you and me home from the hospital. We had no holiday invitations, there were no callers at our door, and the phone was silent. Christmas dinner was a can of Dinty Moore Beef Stew and a loaf of white bread. (Your father had mastered Intermediate Oatmeal, but he had little experience in Foods for Special Occasions.) Yet it was the most memorable Christmas in my life—just because you were there.

After seven or eight short weeks, you began going to your "sitter" early every morning for a couple of months while I returned to my job. I never doubted that you were well cared for, but if I could do it again, I'd stay home and care for you myself. I missed some precious days and weeks with you.

Soon I "retired." We got reacquainted, you and I, and became constant companions as we learned about life from each other. You were quick to learn, and before the age of three you were trotting across the road alone to spend parts of many days with our neighbor. Though I was concerned that you would be a nuisance there, I was assured that "she's no bother—she just does whatever I'm doing."

Then there was Sunday school, and kindergarten, and you went eagerly and naturally without even glancing backward, it seemed. As the years came, you seemed to thrive on new horizons.

Your talents are many, and I rejoice at your willingness to develop and share them. Apparently you understand that "to whom much is given, from him much will be required." Among your talents is a generous supply of uncommon commonsense, and I think you know that wisdom is greater than knowledge.

Soon you'll finish high school and go on to college to continue discovering yourself and your talents and what you can do to build a successful life. I hope you'll remember that *real success is being where God wants you.* Keep asking the Lord where He wants you and how to get there.

When a room in a college dormitory has become your home, I'll grieve a little, I know, but that's as it should be. Though you're abundantly creative, your interest in house-cleaning leaves something to be desired, and your room is often a mess. Still, I don't mind (much) because I know the day is too soon coming when I'll go up to that room, sit on your bed, and wish you were there.

But I'll be happy that you're going onward, opening new doors even though I can't follow. Go ahead! Be happy in remembering that the Lord is your best Friend—but don't forget your mother.

GOD GIVES YOU THE STRENGTH
Dear Maureen:

It's been rough, hasn't it? The operations, the braces, the nauseating kidney x-rays, the steps and stares....

But you've never complained. Not once. I've seen you depressed and maybe you felt like complaining, yet I know no one who is as patient, cheerful, helpful, and forgiving as you are. Sometimes I wonder if you're an angel in disguise.

It looks like the worst is behind us; things are getting better. You can park that wheelchair most of the time now, and you can even manage some stairways if you have to. Soon you'll be out of school and going on to train for a job. I think it's time I shared with you one sentence that has kept me going through all our difficulties. Let me back track a moment.

When you were only about twenty-four hours old, the reality of your "problems" had really hit me, and I was feeling low, to say the least. "Open spine ... won't have normal use of her lower body," the doctor had said. I had whispered, "God, help me," and was sobbing quietly into my pillow when someone came to the side of my bed. He said he was a doctor, and after asking a few questions, he spoke one simple sentence that I've never forgotten: "If the Lord didn't know you could take care of her, He wouldn't have given her to you this way."

I never saw that doctor's face, and I forgot his name before the day was over, but he was one of the most important people I ever "met."

Reen, just remember this: If the Lord hadn't known *you* could handle it, He wouldn't have let you have the burden. He never allows a burden without supplying the strength to carry it.

You were never more happy or excited than you were the day you publicly affirmed your faith in Jesus Christ. Hold onto Him, and He'll never let you fall.

DAD'S RIGHT-HAND MAN

Dear Ross,

You're one of those fortunate few who were born neat—but not too neat. The rest of us are still working at it. You came into the world with your hair combed neatly in place, and neatness has been your inclination ever since.

I once overheard your grandmother telling someone that I always had your hair combed so nicely. I didn't tell her your front cowlick should get the credit. You hate it now, but that cowlick is a symbol of some of your talents—neatness, self-discipline, and organization.

Way back when you could scarcely say the word, you said you were going to be a "fah-muh" like your daddy when you grew up. It looks like you knew what you were talking about.

Now you even say you'd rather do chores after school than play football or basketball. When Dad has been under the weather you've willingly gone out to do the early-morning chores before school—even though it meant taking another shower before you got on the schoolbus.

Your dad is needing a good right-hand man more and more, and it looks like he's got one in you. Farming's a good life, Son. It was the first profession in Creation, and I expect it will endure the longest.

And by the way, you can have the lease on your room as long as you want it.

THURSDAY'S CHILD: THE QUARTERBACK
Dear Todd,

It surprised me not at all when you were chosen starting quarterback this year. We all know you've had enough practice, don't we?

For a long time you didn't realize that your father was watching from a distance while you ran one-man scrimmages, playing all positions, including waterboy—even suffering injury in some of the more crucial plays. When he let you in on the secret that he knew *your* secret passion, you laughed about it. You were resilient enough to laugh at a joke on yourself. That's you. Resilient.

Being "talented" at annoying behavior—not necessarily naughty, just somehow annoying—you've probably had more than your share of out-of-patience tongue lashings. But you take them well. In fact, it's enough to make a parent ashamed. You always bounce back without pouting or bitterness.

You're "Thursday's child," and "Thursday's child has far to go." You're going far, Son. I pray that the Lord will light your path and that you'll always be willing to let Him call *all* the plays in your huddles.

MY HIGH-FLYING FREE SPIRIT
Dear Jonathan,

Well, Jonny, what can I say? You probably won't sit still long enough to read this, but please try.

You're a middle child if there ever was one—stuck between four teenagers and three "little kids." That means you can be a little tagalong or a big brother. Both have their advantages, you know.

The "big guys" have already cut a path for

you—maybe not exactly the one you'll want, but it's a start. And you can be the "hero" for the three that are following you. Make a good road. You wouldn't want them to stumble, would you?

I wish we could bottle your energy. I think there could be a real market for it. You might even want to buy it back yourself in four or five years when the lawn needs mowing.

Keep flying, free spirit. Fill up with God's Spirit, and nobody will ever put out your fire.

GOLDEN-HAIRED CHILD OF THE KING
Dear Jennifer,

I wonder if you know how special you are. You came along ten or eleven years after your older sisters, with a trio of brothers in between. Now we know there's nothing wrong with being a *boy,* but it sure was a nice change to have pink sleepers in the laundry again.

And now you're in first grade already! Before we know it, you'll be baking chocolate chip cookies and taking your driver's test. Is there any way we can keep our little girl little? We wouldn't really want to, would we?

You, too, must find your wings. Will you be a baton twirler, a teacher, a mommy, a race car driver?

It doesn't matter as long as you're a child of the King.When He puts a crown on your golden hair, you can do anything, be anything He wants you to be.

But don't hurry away. We still like having you around.

SWEET SUNSHINE

Dear Joshua,

Sometimes we call you Sonny. We should be spelling it *"Sunny."*

We didn't plan to have a little boy named Josh, but you came along anyway—almost mysteriously—on Jennifer's heels.

And what a delight to have you! You're always (well, almost) bouncy and brimming with enthusiasm and smiles; it would take three pages of single-spacing to tell about the sunshine you've brought us. So I'll save that for when you're older and can understand better.

We're *so* glad you came.

THE LITTLEST ANGEL

Dear Rory,

Well, short stuff, you haven't been around long enough to really firm up a reputation for yourself. You completed our family picture just fifteen years and one week, to the day, after your big sister Kim started it. Halfway between her birthday on December 21 and yours on the 28th, is Christmas—Jesus's birthday.

That's the way I like to think of all of you—with Jesus in the middle, watching over you and helping you.

Some day you'll probably learn the Sunday school song that has these words:

"I am Jesus' little lamb,
Very glad at heart I am,
For my Shepherd gently guides me,
Knows my wants and well provides me. . . ."

When you do, take it to heart. Jesus loves you, and so do we.

Love,
Mom

So, Edward Joseph Blumhoefer, put that in your whistle. It's sweeter than I could ever tell.

We know that all things work together for good to those who love God, to those who are the called according to His purpose.

—Romans 8:28

chapter 11.

WHERE'S MARTHA NOW?

Housewifery, if I had it to do all over again, I'd still choose you.

Oh, there are days when, for an Anthony dollar and a moonlight ride through the Suez Canal, I'd turn in my membership card. But all things considered, home is where I want to be. My house is headquarters for all the gifts, privileges, and obligations God has given me. That's where my action is, and I want to be in the middle of it.

Nobody said it would be easy. It isn't. To complicate matters, I entered housewifery as a Martha wanting to be a Mary. Or as a Mary trying to be a Martha. I wasn't sure which, but when I leave this world, I hope to exit as a satisfactory blend of a window-washing Martha and a prayerful Mary.

JOB DESCRIPTION
Housewife/Fulltime:

On-the-job training mandatory.
Study of home economics necessary but need not be done in a classroom.
Selfishness detrimental to job satisfaction.
Working hours long but flexible.
Free time dependent upon own management ability.
Should be able to turn deaf ear to Gloria Steinem.
Ability to pray without ceasing is clearly advantageous.
Remuneration where you find it—in an appreciative husbandly pat on the backside, a toddler's belly laugh, or a teenager's "Thanks, Mom."
Development of personal communication skills highly recommended.
Some days more demanding than others, but heavenly help and forgiveness available on call twenty-four hours a day.
Love of God and respect for His guidelines important if job is to be secure.

HOMEMAKING: A WORK OF LOVE AND JOY

Every applicant or appointee to "Occupation: Housewife" is wise to analyze that word "housewife." There may be some who would have me

140

apologize even for using it—the very sound of it is lonely and depressing to them. "I'm not *married* to my *house*," they say. But the *Random House Dictionary* defines "housewife" as "a woman in charge of a household, esp. a wife who does all or most of the cleaning and cooking in her own household and who holds no other job."

Judging from readings of news items on employment statistics, one could quickly conclude that "Occupation: Housewife" is fast becoming extinct. Yet other statistics will show that roughly thirty percent of the households in the United States are made up of "single earner primary families," that is, families consisting of a father, mother, and children with only one parent employed outside that household.

With nearly sixty million family households in the country, some simple math can bring one to the reasonable conclusion that a *housewife* today has the company—and hopefully, the moral support—of more than seventeen million other women. She's hardly *alone* in her work.

Now let's look at that dictionary definition again. "A woman *in charge* of a household. . . ." In how many other occupations is a woman given so much authority? Where else is she as free to write her own job description? Still, she can face it responsibly or run from it.

Someone has said, "The Lord must love mediocrity because He made so much of it." Really! It seems to me that He produces only excellence. It's when *we* mishandle, misuse, or neglect His creations—or dodge His plans for us—that they become mediocre.

We let housewifery become a mediocre, monotonous task when we fail or refuse to see the nobility of it. When the going gets rough, we submit to fretful frenzy. Or we succumb to the temptation to bail out by literally lying down on the job or by walking out and shutting the door.

If businessmen approached their jobs the same way, this country would have declared bankruptcy long ago. On the other hand, if businessmen conducted their affairs as judiciously and conscientiously as the many God-respecting homemakers I know, they'd have less traffic in their complaint departments.

Housewifery is a specialized form of *homemaking*. Undoubtedly its continuity and tedium are the parts that leave a bad taste in the mouths of women who could be happy cooking, sewing, having babies, entertaining, and shopping, if it just weren't for the dishes to wash, seams to rip and redo, diapers to wash, more dishes to wash, and the oftentimes limited operating funds of the job.

But then let's consider the "glamorous" surgeon who is always just a slip-of-the-scalpel away from a malpractice suit, the livestock farmer who never quite sees the bottom of the manure pile, even the author whose carefully chosen words can be—and often are—totally and permanently obliterated with one scratch of an editor's blue pencil.

It's easy to lose sight of the royal calling that is ours when we are put "in charge of a household," serving, serving, ever serving. But all of housewifery's "drudgery," all of its "lowliness" should take on a different light when we pause to realize that even the Son of man, our Lord Jesus Christ, came not to be served, but to *serve,* giving even His very life for souls who despised Him.

And today He's the One most willing and able to ease the burden and supposed monotony of housewifery, to raise it to a work of genuine love and joy. According to Psalm 32:8:

> "I will instruct you and teach you in
>   the way you should go;
> I will counsel you and watch over
>   you."

Personally speaking, this gift of God's love and real working presence didn't come as a result of clocking up a certain number of hours doing good deeds to curry His favor or pleading with Him to bail me out of corners. It came as a result of believing in who He is, what He has done, and what He can and will do. It came in simply letting Him take over, in making myself available to Him, just as I am, every day. Therein is real fulfillment, real meaning, real unshakable *joy.* And it's available to anyone and everyone just for the asking.

The Lord has been my Teacher, my Shoulder to cry on, my Helper, my Forecaster, my Dream-painter, my Sounding Board, my Editor, and my Friend.

And fortunately, He's not finished with me yet.

> I love the Lord, for He heard my
>   voice;
> he heard my cry for mercy.
> Because He turned His ear to me,
>   I will call on Him as long as I live.
>   —Pslam 116:1,2

SOME AFTERTHOUGHTS

I see the following as the most important pegs on which blessed housewifery hangs:

1. *Dressing for the job.* A neat, reasonably attractive personal appearance is one of the basics of a productive attitude on any job. Housewifery is no exception. Comfortable, good-fitting, durable, washable clothing is a must for a professional approach to the job.

My work uniform is invariably a pair of comfortable jeans or slacks (preferably free of patches) and a nonbinding top (my best ones have pockets—for the marbles and paper clips and little treasures that cross my paths). Perhaps most important of all is a pair of *good, comfortable shoes,* because when the feet ache, the whole body protests. Gone are the days when I "made do" with $3.99 sneakers. Now I gladly pay $25 or more for wedge cushion-sole oxfords with leather uppers. I think I'm worth it. Absorbent foot-socks complete my underfooting.

2. *Knowing the job.* Consider all facets of the giant challenge that is housewifery. Study them—cleaning techniques, storage needs, marketing, meal planning, hospitality, how to play with children, etc. Don't assume that your mother's or your neighbor's way of doing things is the only way. You may be marching to a different drummer. And contrarily, bear in mind that your mother or neighbor, through their own experiences, may have learned things that you can benefit from.

Here are some books that can help:

The I Hate to Housekeep Book, by Peg Bracken (New York: Fawcett World Library, 1977). Available in paperback or hard cover.

How to Clean Everything, by Alma Chestnut Moore (New York: Simon and Schuster, 1971).

Open Heart, Open Home, by Karen Burton Mains (Elgin, Ill.: David C. Cook, 1976).

3. *Choosing your league.* What is the wisest set of standards for your present situation? If you have a babe in arms and a toddler to nourish, are you going to try to keep up with your sister whose youngsters are school-bound five days a week, or with your empty-

nested mother-in-law? Decide, with your family's help, what should have top priority, remembering that priorities should change as circumstances do.

4. *Planning*. Satisfying accomplishment is the primary goal of organization. Don't be bound to a rigid schedule, but make a rough outline that includes all the basics of your job—allowing leeway for the necessary "interruptions" and the little "surprises" that the Lord might wish to throw your way.

As an illustration, I supply here my own such plan. This is a different outline than I would have used ten, five, or even *one* year ago, and perhaps different than the one I'll need a year from now.

LIST A: DAILY SCHEDULE

6:00-6:30	Personal grooming and meditation (see page 23).
6:30-7:00	Pack school lunches and make breakfast.
7:00-7:25	Breakfast and last-minute school needs.
7:25	School bus!
7:30-8:00	Tidy kitchen, bathroom and bedrooms (children—except youngest—are responsible for their own).
8:00-9:00	Dress Rory, tidy living room, play with Rory (with Captain Kangaroo's company).
9:00-10:00	Kitchen/laundry job of the day (cleaning, ironing, mending, sewing or baking, as needed).
10:00-12:00	Writing, planning, or other paper work.
12:00-1:30	Lunch and nap time.

1:30-4:00	Job of the day and/or social activity (see List B).
4:00-5:30	Open for miscellaneous (including piano lessons and other chauffeuring).
5:30-7:00	Supper (served at 6:15).
7:00-10:00	Family time or church and community activities, done simultaneously with laundry as needed.

LIST B: JOB OF THE DAY

Monday:	Grocery shopping.
Tuesday:	Clean living room.
Wednesday:	Job of the *Week* (see List C).
Thursday:	My day off—no special job of the day.
Friday:	Clean bathroom and bedrooms.
Saturday:	Wash bed linens and clean kitchen (A.M.). Clean living/dining room (P.M.). Family activities.

LIST C: JOB OF THE WEEK
(ON FOUR-WEEK CYCLE)

Week One:	Accounting and bill paying.
Week Two:	Sewing.
Week Three:	Cleaning refrigerator and range.
Week Four:	Clean closets, drawers, cupboards.

5. *Following through.* It's one thing to plan; it can be quite another to carry out the plans. It's more than a

148

matter of physical energy and mental perseverance. In my personal library, I have the works of a number of authors who have dealt with energy, self-discipline and self-understanding in ways that can be especially helpful to "employees of housewifery."
Some of them are:

The Disciplines of the Beautiful Woman, by Anne Ortlund (Waco, Texas: Word, 1977).

What Wives Wish Their Husbands Knew About Women, by Dr. James Dobson (Wheaton, Ill.: Tyndale, 1975).

The Helper, by Catherine Marshall (Waco, Tex.: Chosen Books, 1978).

Spirit-Controlled Temperament, by Tim LaHaye (Wheaton, Ill.: Tyndale, 1966).

6. *Refusing to be hornswoggled by your environment.* If your house, your neighborhood, your family life isn't the way you think you would like it, there's probably *something* you—and the Lord—can do about it.
Here are some resources for further reading in this area:

Home and Yard Improvement, by Midwest Planning Service. Order from Bulletin Room, University of Minnesota, St. Paul, Minnesota 55108. Cost: $3.12.

The section on "Functional Storage" from *Home Management Is,* by Esther Crew Bratton, Ginn and Co., Lexington, Masschusetts 02173.

To Be A Mother, by Ruth Vaughn (Nashville: Thomas Nelson, 1978).

You and Your Child, by Charles R. Swindoll (Nashville: Thomas Nelson, 1977). (This, incidentally, is the very best book on "parenting" I've ever read.)

It may seem strange that I mention the last two books here in the same breath with references on home and yard improvement, but parent-child relationships and one's attitude toward being a parent are a *very real* part of a home's environment.

7. *Getting a hold on your resources of time, money, and energy.* Bodily energy is a tangible scientific resource. Time is fleeting but dependable. Money is an obvious material resource, but too often we overlook or ignore the spiritual elements of resource management. Two excellent books on the subject are:

How to Succeed with Your Money, by George Bowman, rev. ed. (Chicago: Moody Press, 1974).

Your Money Matters, by Malcolm MacGregor and Stanley Baldwin (Minneapolis: Bethany Fellowship, 1977).

8. *Giving thanks to the God who made you and who stands so willing to sustain you.* When we turn our-

selves to Him without reservation, when we open the door to let His love and mighty hands reach in, He works everything—good and bad—together for some magnificently exciting results.